D0492099

The Best of
Morecambe & Wise
A Celebration

The Best of Morecambe & Wise

A Celebration

Eddie Braben

Virgin

Scripts first published by Woburn Press in 1974.

First published in this form by
Virgin Publishing Limited
Thames Wharf Studios
Rainville Road
London W6 9HT

A catalogue record for this book is available from the British Library.

ISBN 1 85227 835 8

Designed by Design 23, London.
Printed and bound in Great Britain by WBC Book Manufacturers Limited.

Contents

Introduction

by Eddie Braben

When Eric and Ernie read any of my scripts for the first time they were like inquisitors – every word, every line was scrutinised. My work had never been examined with such intensity. So much so that sometimes I thought they were looking at death sentences. This was the part of my job that I did not like one little bit, this almost brutal exploration of weeks of work. Quite honestly I couldn't have felt more uncomfortable, more unnerved, if they had been interrogating my own children. An exaggeration? I suppose so.

In fairness it must be said that Eric and Ernie must both have felt more than a little apprehensive: a great deal depended on what I had written on those thirty sheets of foolscap paper. I could see the concern, the uncertainty, etched on both their faces as they picked up page one.

For ever will I remember the first script that I ever presented to Eric and Ernie. It was in Bill Cotton's office at BBC Television Centre in the glorious spring of 1968.

This first script had to be good. If it wasn't, then all Bill's efforts in bringing us together would have been for nothing.

'Eric, Ern, will you at least smile, please?' The smiles did come. Eric laughed; he laughed so much that he had to take his steamed-up glasses off and give them a wipe. Dear Bill Cotton was beaming. Ernie looked very pleased, very relieved. I sat in total disbelief. Even now I find it difficult to appreciate just how gifted and how enormously popular Morecambe and Wise were.

Quite recently when I was told that the Morecambe & Wise Show had been voted the most popular comedy show in television history, it was just staggering. What I don't find difficult to appreciate is the fact that I had the privilege of working with two very dear friends who made a monumental contribution to British comedy.

It's my sincere wish that the book will show how superbly they made that contribution.

Who's Who?

MORECAMBE, *Eric:* not his real name. Took his stage name from his home town of Eric in Lancashire. Educated at Milverton Street School and held the unique honour of being the only pupil ever to obtain 12 A Levels in Abstenteeism. With the outbreak of World War Two he served with great distinction behind the bacon counter at the Co-op, disguised as a middle-aged spinster. Worked down a coal mine where every shift he was carried in a cage to the coal face – if he turned green and fell off the perch all the other miners made a rush for the surface. Got his first break just above the ankle at the Central Pier, Birmingham, after doing the gag about the three Irishmen who wanted to start a one-man band. d. 1984 (but don't tell the BBC – Royalties department still hasn't noticed).

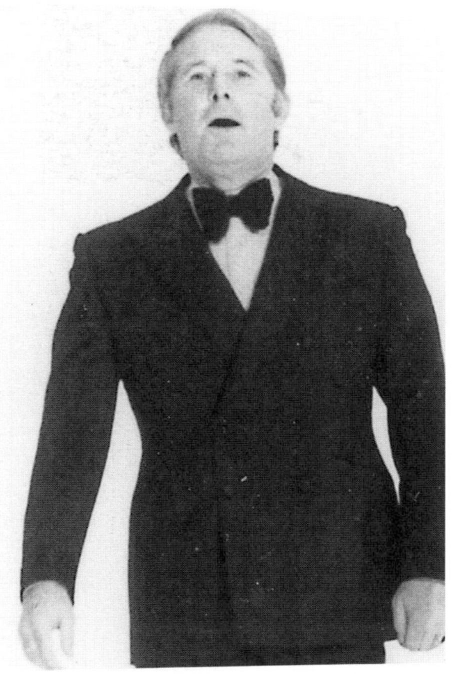

WISE, *Ernie:* real name Lloyd Buttocks. Little can be said of this man that hasn't already been said by people who ought to have more respect. A man of great ingenuity, which showed itself during the Potato Famine of '35 when he invented plastic chips. Also educated at Milverton Street School where he learnt to read French and many other words besides. It was at Milverton Street School that he first showed his propensity and had to stand behind the blackboard for two hours. In 1945 he went to Hollywood and starred in many jungle films playing the part of Tarzan's left leg. Made his first stage appearance at Llandudno in *Cinderella* where he is still remembered as the finest pumpkin they ever had. Asked to name his favourite author, he smiles and with great and understandable pride shows you a signed photograph of himself.

Braben, *Eddie:* he was born. This is confirmed because he has been seen in Liverpool disguised as a human being. The house that he was born in has been purchased by the National Trust as a donkey sanctuary.

Always the adventurer, young Braben ran away from home when he was ten and joined the library. Left school with four 0 levels and an A level. He was the only boy in

his class with an 'Ooooa!' Did his two-year National Service working in the cook-house as a dishwasher: 'The only way I could be sure of getting plenty to eat.' Followed this with four years as a greengrocer and disliked it intensely: 'I should have been at home with all those nuts.'

He really did get the autographs of John Mills and Joan Greenwood on a brown paper bag! Sold his first joke to Charlie Chester for 2s 6d. A telephone call in 1969 from Bill Cotton started what has been called 'The Golden Triangle': Eric Morecambe, Ernie Wise and Eddie Braben. 'If I wrote a good script they made it brilliant.'

Married Deidre, an ex-George Mitchell singer, when she was appearing in *The Ken Dodd Laughter Show* at Liverpool's Royal Court Theatre. Graham, Jane and Clare make up the Braben household. Winner of the Writer's Guild of Great Britain Award for the Best British Light Entertainment Script in 1969, 1970, 1971, 1973. Also in 1973, he won the Writer's Guild Award for the Best British Radio Comedy Series – for *The Worst Show On The Wireless.* Held jointly with Eric and Ernie the Society of Film Television Artists 1972 award for an outstanding contribution to television.

When he grows up he wants to own a ukulele factory. 'There are millions of people in the world who have never owned a ukulele; many of them don't even know which end to blow down.'

We doff our hats to this wonderful man of vision.

The behind-the-scenes genius of these programmes when they first went out was their producer, John Ammonds. He first worked with the boys in the fifties when he was a sound radio producer at BBC Manchester. He started off in broadcasting comedy as a sound effects man for the evergreen ITMA programmes. In spite of his nostalgia for the early days of modern comedy, he was acutely conscious of the need to develop the Morecambe & Wise Shows so that they would remain the most successful comedy series. It was he who first suggested asking celebrities like Glenda Jackson to appear on the show, and was responsible for the improvised Groucho walk which became the well-known Eric and Ernie dance.

The Opening Spot

The most important part of any show that we did was the opening spot. It set the standard for the rest of the comedy content. Either it proved a confidence booster for Eric and Ernie, or it left them more than a little apprehensive, and if it didn't work I could be found quaking in the corridor outside the studio.

Those last couple of minutes standing at the side waiting to go on were always, despite the years of experience, charged with nervous tension. Ernie would go very quiet while Eric would pace up and down clicking his fingers and whistling the signature tune of *Housewive's Choice.*

When I asked him why he did this he was rather surprised because he didn't realise that he did. Of the two, I would say that Eric appeared more nervous. He once said to me that he felt like John Wayne riding out of the fort to fight the Indians. Thankfully all the 'Indians' they faced were friendly. They both liked it if I could write an opening that required a prop, something that could be carried. Eric in particular

was very fond of this device: I suppose it acted as a sort of lifebelt. He was delighted with one opening spot that required him to use an amplified loud hailer and he used it all day long in the studio even in normal conversation. We did have jolly fun.

As I remember, the reason for using the loud hailer was to whip up public support for the 'Save Little Ern' campaign. It went something like this.

Eric *(Through loud hailer)* Now hear this, you will not lay a finger on little Ern. You will leave this building in an orderly manner. Police vehicles are waiting outside to take you to a place of entertainment.

Ernie What are you doing?

Eric You, Ern. You are an endangered species. How many are there of you left?

Ernie There's only me.

Eric Exactly. You have to be preserved.

Ernie Preserved?

Eric Like a small jar of marmalade.

The gentle jibes at Ernie flowed, and were all blasted at him and the audience through the loud hailer. A good night for ad-libs.

The Play What Ern Wrote

To see Morecambe without Wise would be like looking at Blackpool without the tower. No Eric and Ern 'Best Of' would be acceptable, certainly not to me, without a flat sketch and Ern writing yet another play.

The two of them trapped in the flat will forever be my favourite Morecambe and Wise situation. We join them with Ern tapping two-fingered at the typewriter.

Eric Another masterpiece?

Ernie I suppose so. This is the most difficult play I have ever written, it's taken me almost twenty minutes.

Eric Have you ever thought about writing a full-length epic for the screen?

Ernie Tomorrow.

Eric I'm sure you will. The talent was always there even as a lad. Remember that composition you wrote at school?

Ernie It was all about 'My Pet'. The poodle we used to have at home.

Eric Sad that was. I cried when Miss read it out to us.

Ernie It was very sad.

Eric The way it died after biting your Auntie May. How many awards have you won this year?

Ernie Thirty-seven.

Eric Including Crufts? Ern, I think that the time has come for you to accept a challenge.

Ernie A challenge?

Eric Write a musical play, there's money in it. Just look how well Agatha Mitchell has done out of *The Black and White Mousetrap.*

Ernie That's been running now for twenty years.

Eric They got through two hundred and forty-two usherettes.

Ernie Do you think I could write a musical play?

Eric You, Ern, could become another Lionel Burke.

Ernie Bart.

Eric Has he? I didn't know that. Look what *The Sound of Music* did for Eamonn Andrews.

Ernie Julie Andrews.

Eric You know him better than I do. *Showboat*. That was a great musical. Who could ever forget Dame Flora Robson standing on that bale of hay and singing 'Old Man River'? Write a musical this afternoon about Lew Grade: *Promises Promises*.

Ernie It's been done.

Eric Not by him it hasn't.

Ernie Write a musical? I'm sure I could do it. Eric, are you looking at something interesting out of that window?

Eric I'm just a simple fellow.

Ernie That's true.

Eric But to me that is the most beautiful sight that any man could ever wish to see. Ern, that is breathtaking.

Ernie What is?

Eric Ada Bailey hanging out her knickers on the clothes line.

Ernie Come away from that window.

Telephone ringing, Ern lifts receiver.

Ernie Hello. Ernie Wise here ... You're a fellow writer? Gosh!! I'm a fellow writer as well ... I'm going to write a musical this afternoon, if it doesn't rain. You live in the same block of flats? So do I. Why don't you come over for a little chat? ... Splendid, look forward to meeting you.

Eric Fellow writer?

Ernie Lives in the same block of flats.

Eric So do you.

Ernie I told him that. He's coming over to meet me, he's a poet.

Eric I used to fancy myself as a poet.

Ernie You write poetry? You couldn't leave a note for the milkman.

Eric Monologues. I do a lot of those. There used to be a fellow on the musical halls years ago named Tony Bennett. 'Almost a Gentleman'.

Ernie Billy Bennett.

Eric Could you wish for anything more poetic than this? Just listen to how this scans.

Digging for grapes with a bicycle lamp.
By the light from his lantern jaw ...

Eric is interupted by the doorbell ringing.

The bells just gone,
Don't stand there,
There's somebody at the door.

Ernie Rubbish that is. Answer the door.

Eric opens the door. A very effeminate man enters.

Man Hello to you, old fellow.

Eric Can I help you, Miss?

Ernie You're the fellow who lives across the way, you called a few minutes ago.

Man Yes. I thought I'd give you a ring.

Eric I hope you'll both be very happy together.

Ernie My name's Ernie Wise, playwriter. Please sit down.

Eric Take the weight off your mascara.

Ernie I didn't quite get your name.

Man Adrian, Adrian Fondle.

Eric Sounds like a new bra.

Man That's my pen name. My real name is Adrian Caress.

Ernie Do tell about the poems what you're writing, Adrian.

Man Well ...

Eric I do a bit of poetry writing.

Man Really. How so terribly fascinating.

Eric I've just finished one called 'The Fairy'. Nothing personal. My forte is monologues, I've got forty monologues in the next room.

There's a hell of a smell in Dingley Dell,
The fairies are washing their socks,
When up jumps a sailor ...

Ernie Why don't you shut up! Spoil everything you do! I'm sorry about this, Mr ...

Man Call me Adrian.

Ernie Call me Ern.

Eric Call me tomorrow, I've had enough of this.

Going for a Quick One

Once again a prop featured strongly in this opening which was an affectionate send-up of a very popular antiques programme of the day called *Des O'Connor*. No, that's not true. The programme was called *Going for a Song*. It was hosted by a very genial expert with a name I was more than grateful for: Arthur Negus, a very kind man who answered all the questions Eric and I put to him about clocks. We were both collectors. Eric was very enthusiastic when he told me about a clock he'd found half hidden away at the back of one of his favourite antique shops in Harpenden. The owner of the shop told Eric that the clock was over a hundred years old, but that it was also broken, black and rusty and he could have it for a fiver.

Eric bought it and told me with considerable pride that he had been working on the clock for a couple of hours a day for the past three weeks. 'You should see it now.' I was impressed and a touch jealous. When I asked 'What's it like?' he replied, 'Broken, black and rusty'.

Incidentally, I put that line in about Des because I was astonished that we had done a routine about antiques without mentioning him. The Des O'Connor insult gags all came about because in the early days I was looking for the right personality for Eric to joke about, and it had to be someone who was very, very popular. I chose Des because at that time nobody was doing gags against him, he was one of the most popular entertainers in the business, my wife Deidre adored him and he sang!

The very first in a catalogue of Des insult gags was, I think, this one.

Eric I've just bought Des O'Connor's new album.

Ernie Where from?

Eric Boots the chemist.

Ernie Did you need a prescription?

Eric I had to go to the poison counter.

That may or may not have been the first Des O'Connor insult gag. It certainly wasn't the last. When I eventually met Des he shook me warmly by the hand, not the throat, as I thought he might. He was very sincere when he thanked me, saying that it was publicity he could never have bought. Also that his family watched the shows and were very disappointed if Eric and Ernie didn't insult him. I don't think that they were ever disappointed. I'm quite sure that they weren't disappointed when all three finally came face to face.

Eric He's arrived.

Ernie Who?

Eric Do you scare easily?

Ernie I watch *Crossroads*.

Eric Then I can tell you that he's arrived.

Ernie Who?

Eric I'll give you just a little clue ... Des O'Connor.

Ernie He's in the building?

Eric Yes.

Ernie Are you sure?

Eric When the guard dog tries to throw itself off the roof Des O'Connor must be in the building.

Ernie He'll want to sing one of his songs.

Eric I want to marry Raquel Welch but some things just aren't possible.

Ernie God! He's coming!

Ernie Oh. Ladies and gentlemen, a great personal friend of ours, Des O'Connor.

Ernie Des, it's a joy to see you.

Eric Good old Des. Lovely to meet you at long last.

Des Thank you, boys. I take it then that I am going to sing?

Ernie Sing?

Des Yes. I'm going to sing.

Eric Well, with practice I'm sure one day you will.

Des, after some rather devious manoeuvres, did sing. It was a song from his one-man show, and it isn't easy singing a song with only one man in the audience.

Time we joined Eric and Ernie's antique antics with Arthur Negus.

Eric is carrying a box made of antique-looking wood.

Ernie Good evening, ladies and gentlemen, and welcome to the show. What's in that box?

Eric He just gave it to me now.

Ernie Who?

Eric The antique expert in the next studio. Arthur Negligee.

Ernie You mean Arthur Negus.

Eric Yes, I was in the studio next door watching him doing his antique programme. Thought I might pick up a few jokes.

Ernie You're not short of antique jokes.

Eric Is that it?

Ernie So you met Arthur Negus.

Eric Yes, I always get confused between him and the one who married Herbert Wilcox.

Ernie Anna Neagle.

Eric I am glad ... Herbert Wilcox's wife Arthur Negus was in the studio next door, recording the antique programme *Going for a Quick One.*

Ernie *Going for a Song.*

Eric He sings as well? I didn't know that.

Ernie You're interested in antiques?

Eric You've seen the wife.

Ernie Arthur Negus was on the panel.

Eric Yes, but his doctor said he could work. Arthur looked at the first object and he said without a moment's hesitation – That statue is at least five hundred and sixty-seven years old'.

Ernie And was it?

Eric No. It was Max Robertson fast asleep in the chair.

Ernie Who was the guest celebrity?

Eric I'd rather not say because he did make a fool of himself and I don't wish to embarrass the man because I've nothing against Des O'Connor.

Ernie Was he any good?

Eric No idea about antiques. He looked at the object, smiled that smile of his, did forty-five songs and half a joke then said 'I would say that this object is a pair of stone-age jockey shorts.'

Ernie He guessed wrong?

Eric A mile out.

Ernie But the expert told him what it was.

Eric Yes, the expert – Arthur Nuisance.

Ernie Negus.

Eric He picked the object up and he said, almost with contempt, that expression on his face.

Ernie Wrinkles his nose up when he's looking at it.

Eric So do I.

Ernie What did he say it was?

Eric You'll be amazed when I tell you. It's in this box.

Ernie What is it?

Eric Only one of its kind left in the world.

Ernie What is it?

Eric You won't believe me when I tell you what this is.

Ernie What is it?

Eric Only one of its kind left.

Ernie You've said that. What is it?

Eric Would you like to know what it is? This, Ern, this believe it or not was made in the late seventeenth century. It is a genuine Jacobean TV set.

Ernie A Jacobean television set!

Eric Given to me by Arthur Nugget.

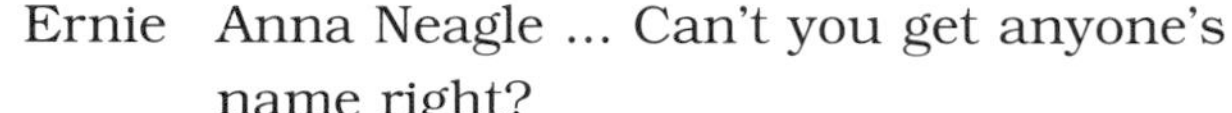

Ernie Anna Neagle ... Can't you get anyone's name right?

Eric I'm sorry, Herbert.

Ernie That's a Jacobean television set?

Eric Yes.

Ernie I suppose you're going to tell me it's in working order?

Eric Do you know what I'm going to tell you?

Ernie No.

Eric It's in full working order. I'll show you. Switch on first. *(Presses button on front of set and raises aerial. Opens the little doors. Opens doors of the set: inside we see a picture of Eric and Ern.)* It's them again!

Ernie They're never off.

Eric I like the one with the glasses. I can't stand the other fellow.

Ernie They're good though, aren't they?

Eric One of them is.

Exits with set.

Frank Finlay

Apprehension, trepidation and a small panic attack when Ernie was told that Frank Finlay was to appear in a Casanova sketch. He wasn't too happy about this as he had seen Frank in the lead role of Casanova in the television series.

Eric and I tried to convince him that it was all very harmless and nobody could possibly take offence, but Ern, of the short legs and high morals, was not impressed. I've seen him with ladies and he's got no disrespect. I've watched him as he tramples over their flower beds and nibbles the cherries. As far as I'm concerned, he's too fond of the 'forbidden fruit'. Eric didn't say a word, he just sat there eating an apple.

When Ernie read the script he was shocked, stunned and horrified when he saw that he was to play the female lead opposite this lecher.

'No! No! No! I would lose my dignity.' There was an answer to that which Eric held back because he wanted the sketch to go ahead. It was obvious that Ern was against the idea for one very good reason: he didn't want to upset his fan, despite the fact that we assured him that Cyril, his hairdresser admirer in Carlisle, would understand that Ernie was a professional and had a job to do. What finally decided him to do the sketch was when we told him that a potion would be surreptitiously deposited in Frank's coffee before the sketch began. Ernie was quite satisfied with this after he had looked up 'surreptitiously' in the dictionary. Something went very wrong with the plan: just seconds before the Casanova sketch started I fell asleep.

Ernie Ladies and gentlemen, it's time to meet our special guest. Star of the sensational BBC series *Casanova*, Mr Frank Finlay ... Mr Finlay welcome to the show. And I know that you are going to enjoy working with me.

Frank Still as modest as ever: I'm going to enjoy working with both of you.

Eric enters and speaks to Ernie.

Eric Don't let it throw you, but there's a drunk from the audience standing right next to you. I knew we'd have trouble. They're a vicious lot out there tonight. *(To Frank)* Excuse me, sir. You're not allowed in front of the cameras. We've got a famous guest star coming on in a minute.

Starts to rush Frank off and Frank lunges back at Eric.

Eric *(getting behind Ernie)* Hey, any more of that and I'll throw him at you.

Ernie Eric, please. This is Mr Finlay, our guest star. Mr Finlay, Eric Morecambe.

Eric I do apologise, sir. Mistook you for one of the audience. Sorry about the fracas. *(Speaking to off-stage)* It's all right to say fracas, isn't it ... No, fracas. They're looking it up. It's all right for me to say fracas.

Frank Pleased to meet you, Eric.

Ernie Frank is our special guest. *(Quietly to Eric)* Picked a good 'un this week.

Eric How did you know he was my favourite?

Frank Did you say ... did you say I was your favourite?

Eric Only watched you week in and week out without fail.

Frank Gosh! You've had world-famous people on your shows and you didn't say that to any of them.

Eric My number one you are. The minute your programme started I got all excited. I'd shout to Ern – 'It's on, Ern'. *(Starts*

singing signature tune to Dr Finlay's Casebook*)* What I want to know is, when are you and Janet coming back with another series?

Frank *(looking disappointed)* You did say ... *(Sings signature to tune* Dr Finlay*)*

Eric That's the one ... My favourite you are.

Ernie *(To Eric)* Do you want to have a word with me?

Eric No.

Ernie I want to have a word with you. *(To Frank)* Excuse us just a moment. I have to have a word with Dandini. *(Takes Eric aside)*

Eric *(Returning to Frank and taking him by the hand)* My sincere and humble pardon. My associate here has just told me who you are. I'm sorry about the confusion – but it doesn't often happen.

Frank I know that. I've seen all your shows. And you always treat your guests with great courtesy and respect.

Eric *(Aside)* This boy's a fool.

Ernie Well, Mr Finlay, if you'll just go and get changed we'll see you later in the show.

Frank I do apologise for the fracas.

Eric *(To off-stage)* It's all right if he says fracas, isn't it?

Lust Over London

Casanova – Frank Finlay

Moveova – Ernie Wise

Turnova – Eric Morecambe

Serving Wench – Ann Hamilton

Young Rake – Percy Thrower

Spotty Beau – Robin Day

Landlord of the Duck Inn –
Charlie Drake

Scene 1: A private room in a tavern. A serving wench (Ann Hamilton) is placing chairs at a table. Ernie enters as a gentleman of the period. He is carrying a silver-topped cane.

Ernie Hello.

Ann completely ignores Ernie.

Ernie Hello, I say.

Ann What do you want?

Ernie A civil word.

Ann I've yet to meet the man worthy of one.

Ernie I take it that you are the serving wench?

Ann Who might you be in your finery?

Ernie I am Viscount Ern of Peterborough.

Ann You are the one what ordered this private room?

Ernie I'm expecting a friend any minute now. You'll be waiting on us?

Ann Provided you keep your hands to yourself.

Ernie I can assure you that ...

Ann You can assure me of nothing. All you men are the same.

Knock at the door.

Ernie Here's my friend now.

Eric enters, also as a dandy of the period: he is carrying a huge silver-topped cane.

Eric Evenin' all. Sorry I'm late. Eric de Quincey Morecambe, Fourth Duke of Harpenden without Portfolio – but my doctor is working on it. Third in line I am – wish the other two would hurry up, I can't wait much longer. I take it you are the serving hatch?

Ann exits.

Eric What a lovely mover!

Ernie Good to see you, de Quincey.

Looks at Eric through lorgnette on long handle.

Eric Didn't know you were hard of hearing.

Ernie Sit down.

Eric Speak up!

Ernie As you wish.

Eric Half past three.

Both sit down.

Ernie *(Hands note to Eric)* I'd like you to read this. *(Offers his lorgnette)* Perhaps you'd like to use these?

Eric I have my own, thank you.

Takes out a lorgnette stick on the end of which there is a large false nose.

Eric	*(Gasp of horror)* A letter from Casanova.
Ernie	Yes, Casanova. He seeks yet another conquest in this city.

Eric	Not ... not your beautiful twin sister Honour?
Ernie	Yes. My beautiful twin sister Honour.
Eric	Whom tellest you of this and how knowest youm of it?
Ernie	I intercepted a letter what he sent by word of mouth – he has a tryst.
Eric	Then you've nothing to worry about – if he's wearing one of those he won't even be able to stand up never mind anything else.
Ernie	He is meeting my beautiful twin sister this very night in his private chamber upstairs.
Eric	We must get some silver paper and try and foil him ... A Medieval joke!
Ernie	Will you help me?

Eric After that joke I'm the one that needs help. To save Honour's honour, I will, sir.

Ernie Good fellow. *(Shakes Eric's hand)*

Ann enters.

Ann There's a man out here with a funny face.

Eric Tell him we've got one.

Ann He calls himself Casanova and he's got a funny walk.

Frank enters as Casanova: he touches Ann's cheek.

Frank How very charming.

Ann Don't you come that game with me - I hate men.

She exits.

Ernie Mr Casanova?

Frank Viscount Pete of Ernborough?

Ernie No, Viscount Ern of Peterborough.

Eric But you were close ... Eric de Quincey Morecambe, Fourth Duke of Harpenden. *(Bows)* Can you help me?

Frank Delighted.

Ernie Please sit down.

All sit at the table.

Eric Wench!

Ann enters.

Eric Bring three tankards of mead. *(To Frank)* Are you hungry?

Frank Yes.

Eric And one poached swan on toast, and be careful where you put the feathers!

Frank And don't be too long, you exciting woman.

Ernie Tell me, Mr Jackanory - why exactly are you visiting London?

Frank I'll be perfectly frank with you - I have a long-felt want.

Eric There's no answer to that!

Frank I am told that the most beauteous maiden in this city is a Mistress Honour.

Ernie And you intend to ...

Frank I am Casanova and I cannot resist the challenge.

Ernie She is sweet and pure.

Frank Do you know the lady?

Eric/Ernie *(Wink behind Frank)* No.

Ernie Sir, when do you intend to perpetrate this lascivious deed upon the innocence of the sweet Honour?

Frank This very night.

Eric Hellfire!

Ernie May I remind you, sir, that she has had a vicarage upbringing. Her father was the vicar of St Bernard's.

Eric Used to have the collection box hanging round his neck.

Ann enters.

Ann Do you want anything?

Ernie Not now.

Eric and Ernie watch as Frank takes a silver bottle from pocket: he takes a sip then places it back in pocket.

Frank *(To Ann)* Hello.

Ann looks at Frank, then gasps with passion.

Ann Kiss me!

Eric Who's paying for the mead?

Ann *(At door: still stunned)* I'll pay for it myself.

Eric That's very good. You've saved us a tip as well.

Frank I think I curried her favours.

Eric You very nearly casseroled her dumplings.

Frank There you are – you have witnessed Casanova at work.

Frank exits with Ann upstairs.

Ernie He just drank from that silver bottle and the girl went berserk. We've got to get that silver bottle from him before he gets his hands on my twin sister, Honour.

Eric How do we do that?

Ernie Look I've got an idea. You play the part of his manservant and I'll dress up as my twin sister Honour.

Eric I see. I'll play the manservant, but you know what Casanova is like. What happens if he tries to hullo folks and what about the workers?

Ernie What?

Eric What happens if he gets you in his room alone and you are dressed as a woman, and he tries to ...

Ernie I don't understand.

Eric What happens if he pushes you towards the bed and ...

Ernie I don't know what you mean.

Eric If you don't know what I mean you deserve everything you flamin' get!

Scene 2: Casanova's bedroom. Bedroom is dominated by large four-poster bed: bed has curtains drawn around it. Casanova is adjusting his waistcoat and looking in the mirror.

Frank Ah you handsome brute. I fail to see how even the prudent Mistress Honour will be able to resist me. Yes, I think there might well be yet another notch on the bedpost before this night is through. *(Knock at door)* Enter.

Eric enters as manservant.

Frank Who are you?

Eric Your manservant.

Frank I didn't ask for a manservant.

Eric Whether you asked for one or not you've got one.

Frank Just a moment. Haven't I seen you before somewhere?

Eric No, this is my best disguise.

Frank You look like the idiot downstairs.

Eric Was he wearing glasses?

Frank Yes.

Eric Does he have a northern accent?

Frank	He has got a northern accent.
Eric	*(Taking off wig)* Does he look like me?
Frank	Yes, he looked exactly like you – but you've got more hair.
Eric	*(Putting wig back on ... Aside)* We've got a right one here.
Frank	I don't need a manservant.
Eric	A custom in our country. Must have someone to arrange your knick-knacks – I take it you brought them with you?
Frank	No. I am entertaining a lady here this evening.
Eric	In that case you'll need this.

Holds up a scent spray.

Frank	What's that?

Eric No woman can resist this – it's called 'Stallion'.

(Couple of quick sprays)

Frank Is it good, that 'Stallion'?

Eric Tried it out when I was on holiday at Blackpool – a donkey followed me home to the digs. Very powerful stuff this is.

Quickly sprays it around the room and the round wooden knobs on top of the bedposts drop off.

Frank It is indeed most powerful.

Eric Well, there is a frost about. Are *you* all right?

Frank Yes.

Eric Where's the bed?

Frank This is the bed.

Eric Sorry, I thought it was the bandstand. First time I've ever seen a bed with goal posts at both ends.

Eric goes on bed with Frank: jumps up and down.

Eric By golly – it's well sprung.

Frank Thank you for the spray and the scent, I don't think I'll be needing you for the rest of the evening.

Eric The beautiful Miss Honour will be here any moment, sir – you have powder on your waistcoat.

Frank Have I really?

Frank turns his back on Eric to dust off powder: Eric takes an identical silver bottle from his pocket and switches it with the silver bottle in Frank's coat, which is draped over a chair. Places genuine bottle in his own pocket.

Frank Describe Miss Honour to me. Describe her beauties.

Eric I've never seen them, sir. It would only be conjecture on my part. Anyway, if you've seen one you've seen 'em all.

Knock at door.

Eric That'll be him ... or her now.

Crosses to door and opens it.

Eric The beautiful Honour.

Ernie enters as Honour.

Frank Do my eyes deceive me?

Eric The short answer is yes. This is Honour; Honour this is the man who's having trouble with his eyes.

Ernie Charmed.

Eric What do you think?

Frank Even more beautiful than I had imagined.

Eric You're going to be in trouble tonight.

Frank I am Casanova – I have my reputation to consider and I will have my way with the most beautiful woman in London.

Ernie *(Aside to Eric)* He's got his hand on my bottom!

Eric Pretend you don't like it.

They walk over to the bed.

Frank *(To Eric)* I am the greatest lover in the world and she *will* yield.

Ernie *(Getting up)* Please unhand me. I am only a weak, gentle maiden.

Gives Frank an enormous whack.

Frank Oh, I like a woman with spirit. Extreme situations call for extreme measures. *(To Eric)* Where's my silver bottle? *(Returns to Ern, looks at him for a few seconds.)* Hello.

Ernie *(Big smile)* Hello.

Frank *(Puzzled but tries again)* Hello.

Ernie *(Winking and nudging Frank)* Hello.

Eric *(To Frank)* I don't want to worry you but I think you've had it.

Frank In that case I must use force.

Eric Just a moment, I'll give you a hand.

Eric pushes Ern on to bed, Frank and Eric draw curtains. This is followed by much shouting and movement. From behind the curtains –

Ernie Stop that!

Frank Stop what?

Ernie Give over!

Frank Get 'em off!

Ernie/Frank Oooh!!!

Eric What did you think of his acting in that play?

Ernie Whose acting?

Eric Frank Funny.

Ernie Finlay.

Eric I thought it was Funny.

Ernie He gave everything he had in that play.

Eric You don't have to tell me. I was the one who had to carry him back to his digs – and he still owed his landlady for two weeks and she was a big woman.

Ernie I wrote his part that way so he'd be too exhausted to ask about money.

Eric Good lad. How much was he supposed to get?

Ernie It was in his contract.

Eric But he can't read Greek.

Ernie Exactly.

Eric That's what I like about you, you're all wallet.

Ernie True. I should have been an international financier.

Eric You could have been one of the Gnomes of Peterborough.

Ernie That's why this next sketch is one of my favourites.

Eric The Bank Manager Sketch.

Ernie Love anything to do with banks.

Eric I meant to tell you – when you go into Barclays Bank you don't have to light a candle and place it on the counter.

Bed Sketch 1

My favourite sketch? Difficult to pinpoint one in particular. The best answer I can give is that I have always enjoyed writing and watching the performances of flat sketches, particularly bed sketches. The thinking behind placing Eric and Ernie in a double bed was simply that there was no escape. They could speak their innermost thoughts, taunt, jibe and insult each other, something that they would never, never, ever do in front of anyone else.

Some of my favourite lines first made themselves known in bed sketches. Eric looking out of the window and observing, 'Red sky at night means that the shepherd's cottage is on fire.' Still looking out and upwards from the window, 'That's Mars up there, you can see it between meals.' Or the time when a police car went speeding past with its siren sounding, 'He's not going to sell much ice cream going at that speed'. In one of the very earliest bed sketches Eric was reading *The Wind in the Willows* while Ern was creating another masterpiece, his fourteenth that day. After the recording and while still in the bed, Eric wrote inside the book, 'To Eddie. Stolen from BBC Props. June 1979.' I really can't tell you how much that beautiful book means to me.

We did once have a gag in a bed sketch and I believe it was decided to take it out on the grounds that it might have upset animal lovers. If you're an animal lover, look away now.

Eric I've put the cat out.

Ernie What for?

Eric It was on fire.

Possibly, because I liked that gag so much, it might well have been sneaked in somewhere else at a later date. It certainly wasn't Rolf Harris in *Animal Hospital*. Perhaps Trevor Mcdonald did it as an 'And Finally' on *News at Ten*. No, I don't think so.

Ernie-Money

Ernie It's got me beat, I just can't make it out. Just can't understand it at all. The market's down four points.

Eric Got me beat as well. Desperate Dan's just eaten four cow pies – he's still hungry.

Ernie What are you talking about?

Eric In this comic he is, every week. He's just stopped a train with his chin.

Ernie Why don't you grow up? I'm trying to study big business.

Eric A little less lust for money and more fun, that's what we want in the world today.

Ernie So we both read comics and who looks after the financial side of the business? Who pays the bills?

Eric Lend me your pen.

Grabs Ernie's pen.

Ernie No, I'm using it.

Eric You can borrow mine. I want to join the dots up in this comic.

Ernie Join what dots up?

Eric *(Drawing on comic)* You join all the dots up and it makes a picture.

Ernie That must be very difficult.

Eric Not really. I do it every week. Wonder what the picture will be? *(Looks at picture)* That's disgusting, that is. Comics haven't half changed since I was a lad.

Ernie Don't you think that it's about time you grew up and accepted your responsibilities?

Eric *(Picks up a second comic.)* Few more Peter Pans like me and the world would be a happier place.

Ernie Then you read your comics and leave me to attend to business matters.

Eric Great story in this comic, Ern – a topping yarn it says here.

Ernie You read it if it's all that topping.

Eric *(Reading aloud)* Dick D'Arcy stood before the headmaster of St Jim's. 'I give you my word of honour, sir,' he said with his head held high and firmness in

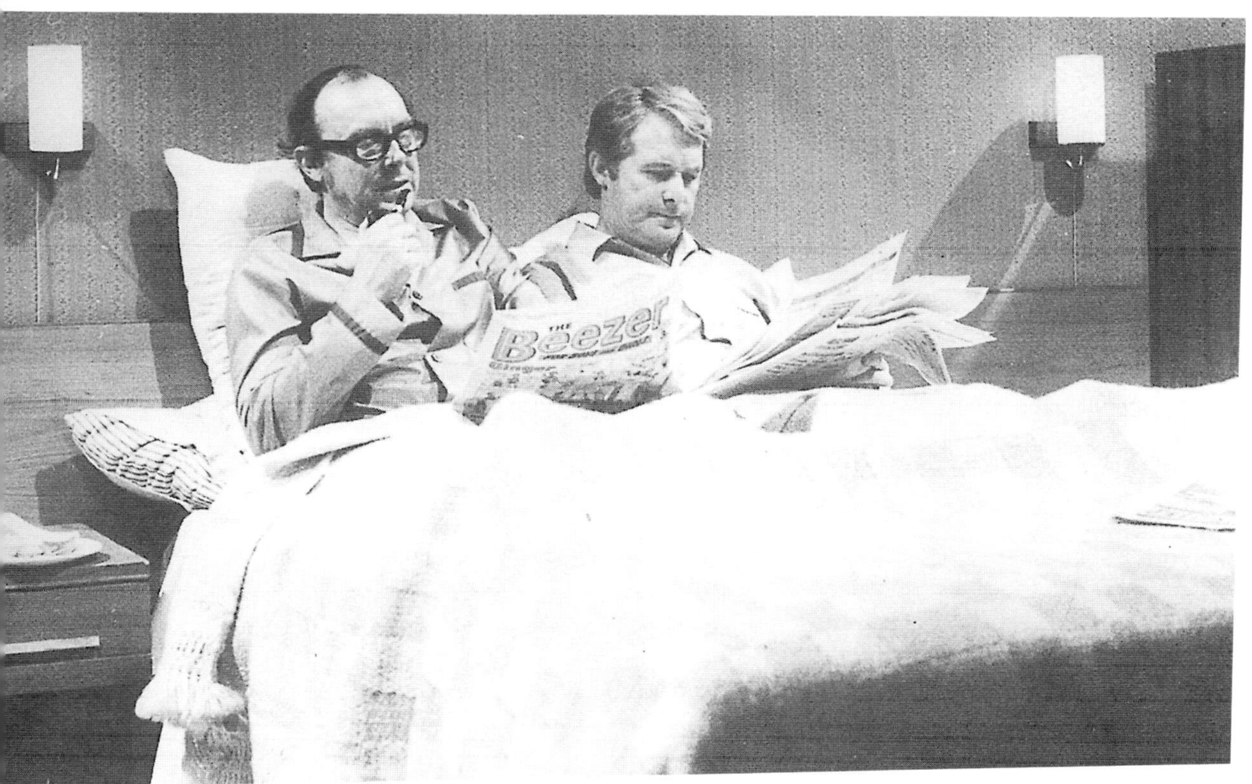

his voice. 'I have no earthly idea how matron's knickers came to be in my school bag.'

Ernie Disgusting. It doesn't say anything like that. Now shut up and leave me to work in peace. I'm engrossed in high finance.

Eric High finance.

Ernie Yes.

Eric With those legs? Impossible. I've been with you when you've gone into the bank, your little head just sticking up over the top of the counter and all the bank clerks whispering to one another – 'Sooty's back'.

Ernie Can I get on with my work?

Eric Call that work? Don't need brains for that.

Ernie In that case *you* should find it very easy. *(Offers paper to Eric) You* sort out the financial side of things.

Eric I'm busy aren't I?

Ernie Reading comics? Ha! You're as thick as a docker's sandwich.

Eric And what does that mean?

Ernie It means that I know. It means don't try and bluff *me*. We went to the same

school, we were in the same class – *I* know.

Eric We're off now are we? Here we go again. 'All Our Yesterdays'. Milverton Street School again?

Ernie Yes, Milverton Street.

Eric Keep bringing that one up when it suits you.

Ernie You're the one making the noise about brains.

Eric Gold stars I got in my sum book off 'Miss'.

Ernie You used to nick them out of her desk at playtime and stick them in yourself.

Eric I didn't. Miss gave them to me. Full of ticks it was, and VGs and nine out of ten.

Ernie I saw what she wrote in your book – she wrote 'You must try harder'.

Eric That was nothing to do with sums – that was personal between me and Miss.

Ernie You were the laughing stock of the class. No wonder I went up to 1A and you went down to 4C.

Eric Read your paper.

Ernie We couldn't wait for Miss to get you to stand up and answer questions. 'Morecambe, where do we get demerara sugar from?' Do you remember what you said? 'From the Co-op, Miss'. *(Laughing)* Oh, dear me.

Eric What about PT then? What about PT matie! Every time we had PT there was that note again from your mother. 'Please excuse Ernest from PT. He has a weak chest and mustn't take his vest off.'

Ernie That's not my fault. Not my fault if I had a weak chest.

Eric It couldn't have been all that weak.

Ernie What do you mean?

Eric I've kept this to myself all these years, but now that the knives are out and fully honed ...

Ernie Go on.

Eric I saw you one playtime behind the bike shed with Rita Greenhough.

Ernie You never saw me behind the bike shed with Rita Greenhough.

Eric It was after that, that I had to start wearing glasses.

Ernie You never saw me behind the bike shed with Rita Greenhough.

Eric I met her last week and she was still laughing.

Ernie You never saw me behind the bike shed with Rita Greenhough. Jealous.

Eric What!

Ernie You were jealous of me at school because I was always better dressed than you.

Eric Ha! Ha! You only started wearing long trousers when your dad went on nights.

Ernie At least my father didn't come home at night and knock my mother about.

Eric Your father didn't dare knock your mother about. Who'd want to tackle King Kong in a pinny?

Ernie This all started just because you know nothing about money matters and investments.

Eric Who doesn't know anything about investments?

Ernie You don't.

Eric I'll show you. *(Takes paper from Ernie)* If you want to invest your money put it in 'Ickey'.

Ernie Ickey? ICI *(Takes paper back from Eric)* Now please, a little peace and quiet? I'm meeting my bank manager in the morning to discuss investments.

Eric You carry on.

Ernie studies the Financial Times.

Ernie EMI looks good.

Eric Can't go wrong there.

Ernie What do you know about it? You don't even know what EMI stands for.

Eric I do.

Ernie What?

Eric Eric Morecambe's Irresistible.

Ernie Read your comic.

Eric Why this sudden interest in stocks and shares and investments all of a sudden? What's wrong with the biscuit tin under the bed?

Ernie Read your comic.

Eric *(Thinks for a second then picks up the* Beano*)* Lord Snooty. *(Laughs)* He's staying with his Aunt Agatha and she's just said to him will ... *(Looks up)* You had an Aunt Agatha. She died about two months ago, didn't she?

Ernie It's got nothing to do with you – that's family business.

Eric *(Slowly realising)* Oooh! A little tickly did you have, eh! Come on. Let's have the truth.

Ernie If you must know, I've had a windfall.

Eric There's some bi-carb in the cupboard. She's left you a few bob then?

Ernie There was a great affection between us – it was a terrible shock to me.

Eric You couldn't stand the sight of her.

Ernie Loved my auntie, I did.

Eric Crawler!

Ernie I didn't crawl at all! You've got to look after yourself in this life.

Eric You must be worth a few bob now then?

Ernie That's my business.

Eric How much did she leave you?

Ernie I'm not saying.

Eric Would you like a piece of my chicken sandwich?

Ernie No. You're not getting any of the money.

Eric You can have the whole of my chicken sandwich if you like, and this glass of milk.

Passes them over to Ernie, who takes them.

Ernie You're not getting any of the money so there's no point in trying to be nice to me. It doesn't suit you.

Eric All right, if that's your attitude I'm going to sleep. Goodnight.

He settles down under the covers. Ernie starts to drink the glass of milk: it sprays out either side.

Ernie You rotten devil!

Eric quietly sniggers to himself.

The Bank Manager

As my mother was only a tiny lady it's understandable that she was fond of saying 'There's good stuff in little parcels'. This was certainly true of my little friend, Ernie Wise MBE, which stands for Member of Barclays Elite, a fitting title as he has always been a prestigious and highly esteemed depositor with that predominant establishment, and Ernie loved banks. Not for him stamp collecting, growing roses or birdwatching. His most treasured possession is, and it's thought to be the only surviving copy, *Bank Managers of the British Isles*.

Ern had met all 35,000 of them and they're logged in his *Eye Spy a Bank Manager Book* given to him as a Christmas gift when he was three years old by his uncle, Scrooge Wise. During one of Ern's meetings with the manager of his local bank, the one with the 'Ernie Wise Wing', he suggested as a rather clever ploy to bring in more investors – the following, all to be held in that particular bank: a guess the weight of the bank manager's wife competition; afternoon tea dances; coffee mornings; and bank boot sales, selling mostly slightly used pinstriped suits, starched white collars, bowler hats and whatever else the female staff had no further use for.

If Barclays wanted to make use of Ernie's ideas he was more than happy for them to do so, for his usual 12 1/2 per cent. One idea that was refused point blank was that Barclays Bank should be the first bank in the UK to provide bed and breakfast accommodation to meet the requirements of overnight bank spotters. Nobody knows just how wealthy Ernie really is. Some indication might come from the time when he accidentally dropped his wallet and Eric claimed that it registered 7.5 on the Richter scale.

Where charitable causes were concerned Ernie was not to be found behind the door. More probably he would be found on his hands and knees hiding under the table. Whenever the Salvation Army lass knocked at his front door and rattled her collection box Ernie didn't hesitate, he flung his door wide open. It opened outwards.

When I told Ernie that I would most definitely be writing a sketch about a bank manager he said 'I'm delighted to hear that', then took his foot off my neck and helped me up. I was inspired to write this saga after I had heard him declare, with a sincerity and emotion that left me quite breathless with admiration: 'When I die you will find 15 per cent per annum engraved on my heart.' It's all so terribly moving.

Scene: Bank manager's office: manager is seated behind his desk. Intercom on desk buzzes: manager presses a button and speaks into it.

Manager Yes, Miss Dunn.

Ann *(Distorted)* There's a Mr Wise and a Mr ... Ooh!

Eric *(Distorted)* Sorry.

Ann *(Distorted)* A Mr Morecambe to see you, Mr Biggs, sir.

Manager You can show them both in.

Ernie Good morning, sir. Eric, this is Mr Biggs.

Eric Mr Biggs. That's a good name for a bank manager.

Manager Will you both take a seat, gentlemen.

Ernie Thank you. *(Sits at desk)*

Eric *(Looking around)* So this is where you do it.

Manager This is where I do it?

Eric Good for you.

Ernie Why don't you sit down and shut up!

Eric *(To manager)* He's talking to you. *(Sits)*

Manager I have your files here. Mr Morecambe and Mr Wise. I'm a very busy man and I would appreciate it if you could tell me what it is you want to discuss with me. *(Looks at wrist watch)* I can let you have two minutes.

Ernie Very well. *(Rises and struts about with some importance)* My rich Aunt Agatha has passed over and left me a substantial legacy.

Manager *(Sudden change of attitude)* A substantial legacy ... a rich aunt ... A cigar, Mr Wise? *(Offers Ern a cigar)*

Eric I have an auntie who isn't feeling too well – perhaps half a cigar?

Eric reaches for cigar: manager shuts box quickly. As Ernie lights cigar, Eric takes it.

Eric Can I have a light?

Manager Now then, Mr Wise, you would like some advice on investments.

Ernie I was thinking about overseas investments.

Eric Swiss banks.

Manager Swiss banks?

Eric Better rate of exchange in Switzerland – you get sixteen yodels to the pound.

Ernie Will you keep out of this?

Manager *(Opens Ernie's file)* Let's see what business interests you have at the moment, Mr Wise.

Ernie I am a playwright of considerable note. For my first business venture I am going to start the Ernest Wise Plays Publishing Company.

Manager What a talented man you are, Mr Wise. I didn't know that you wrote plays.

Eric He only wrote twelve yesterday.

Manager *Twelve* plays?

Ernie There's only one I'm not really happy about.

Eric But he'll finish it today before he has his tea ... *(To Ern)* ... won't you?

Manager So your aunt has died and left you this money.

Ernie I'm her only living relative.

Manager You're quite certain of this?

Eric Positive. I just saw his leg move.

Manager Mr Morecambe, I am trying to discuss business with Mr Wise. *(Looks at file)* I see that you have quite a large annuity.

Eric You can see it from there, can you? He's got a belt at home. I don't know why he doesn't wear it.

Ernie Stop butting in and mind your own business.

Eric Certainly. *(Takes out comic and begins to read)*

Ernie Do you see what I have to put up with, Mr Biggs? A grown man reading comics.

Manager Yes. Let's see how best we can invest your legacy, Mr Wise. *(Looking at file)*

Ernie *(Aside to Eric)* Reading a comic in a bank manager's office.

Eric They're all in here, good they are.

Manager There's International Chemical, Amalgamated Tin ...

Eric Desperate Dan.

Manager *(Still looking at file)* United Steel ...

Eric Pansy Potter.

Manager Bonnie Bluebell ... International Computers ...

Eric Bonnie who?

Manager *(Realising)* Bonnie Bluebell – character from a comic many years ago.

Eric Don't remember that one.

Manager Bonnie Bluebell was a fairy, she broke her wing and a kind lady found her crying underneath a gooseberry bush.

Eric Do that a lot fairies, always breaking their wings, especially when there's a bit of frost.

Manager Now I suggest you invest your legacy in United Steel and Amalgamated Tin and possibly the rest in unit trusts. How much exactly have you to invest?

Ernie Twelve fifty.

Manager Twelve hundred and fifty pounds?

Ernie No. Twelve fifty.

Manager Twelve pounds ...

Ernie And fifty pence.

Eric It would have been fifteen pounds if she'd taken the empties back. She was going to leave it to the Cat's Home but he needs the milk more than they do.

Manager I don't see how we can talk about investing twelve pounds fifty pence. *(Rises)*

Eric Are you going?

Manager *(With sarcasm)* I suggest you put it in a box under the bed.

Eric I told him that. I could have been a manager.

Eric and Ernie go to leave.

Manager Just one moment, gentlemen. I would like to have a word with you, Mr Morecambe. In private.

Eric Anything you say in front of me can be said in front of him, as long as he leaves.

Manager Please sit down. *(They sit.)* It's about your overdraft. I see that you owe the bank ten pounds.

Eric I've no further interest in the matter. If you look at my statement you will see that I have to my credit the sum of one thousand three hundred and seventy-three pounds.

Manager *(Long suffering)* Mr Morecambe, that's the date!

Eric The date?

Manager The first of the third, seventy-three. The important figures are these here printed in red. Looking at your statement, you don't seem to have regular money coming in.

Ernie Well, we don't get paid regularly. We work for the BBC.

Manager The British Broadcasting Corporation?

Eric No, the Birkenhead Brick Company.

Manager What exactly do you do for a living?

Ernie We're just entertainers.

Eric We used to be on the stage before we closed all the variety theatres. We used to do jokes.

Manager Wisecracks?

Eric I'm afraid he does these days. It's his age.

Manager How very curious. I write a few jokes myself.

Eric and Ernie have a horrified reaction.

Manager Would you like to hear one or two?

Both No!

Manager But possibly you could use this one in your act.

Judge in court to prisoner – 'Have you ever been up before me?'

Prisoner – 'I don't know, what time to you get up in the morning?'

He chuckles and looks up, laughing, at the boys. There is no reaction from them and the manager's face becomes serious.

Manager Could I send this to any other comedian?

Ernie Send it to Jimmy Tarbuck.

Manager Jimmy Tarbuck? Would he use my material?

Eric Why not. He uses everybody else's.

Both exit rapidly.

The Bank Manager

New Balls Please

It was a great personal tragedy and an enormous disappointment for the nation when Eric Morecambe had to withdraw from the 1960 Olympic Games in Rome with a dislocated fetlock. That this great athlete would not be competing had deprived Great Britain of at least six gold medals, so he told me. He had good reason to feel bitter after the punishing training he had committed himself to, specially for the high jump. Every morning he had been preparing for this event in a field behind his Harpenden home. He took a 200-yard run with the Pole, then leapt into the air, on occasions reaching a height of 60 feet. Shortly after making one of these prestigious jumps he said 'Even if I don't win a gold medal, I should be able to get into Wembley to see the Cup Final without a ticket.' As a swimmer he is without doubt the best, so he told me. He was determined to become a swimmer, despite a setback at a very early age when a spectator shouted, as Eric dived into the water, 'Who threw those braces in?' As a tennis player, Eric's style was breathtakingly unique, copied by the greatest players in the world, including that lady legend of the courts, Jelly Bean King, so he told me. He was quite thrilled at doing a tennis sketch because, as he said at the time, 'This should prove an inspiration to all youngsters just starting out in the game.' Can anyone doubt that statement? Here is a ball-by-ball replay of what was arguably one of the greatest tennis matches ever screened by the BBC, as Eric takes on his great friend and rival, Ernie Wise.

It should be said that Ernie Wise was no pushover. He was a very fine player who once reached the final of the men's singles mixed doubles for women, so he told me. Credit where credit is due. When the tennis racket is spun to decide who serves, and it breaks, this was Eric's idea. When it came to the question of what to wear it was never asked because we all knew, no matter what the sketch was about, that Eric would wear his beloved suspenders. If you don't want to know the result of this pulsating match, look away now, or whitewash the cat.

Scene: A tennis court, of which we only see the half to the right-hand side of the net. Ernie is waiting with rackets. Eric enters through gate in long shorts.

Ernie Lovely day for it, Eric.

Eric Never mind that, just get on with the game.

Ernie Going to show me a thing or two are you?

Eric Cut the chat and let's get the game going.

Ernie tests the strings on his racket.

Eric What are you doing?

Ernie Testing the strings.

Eric tests his strings: they are very loose.

Ernie Good racket you've got there.

Eric I'll use me championship racket.

Ernie That's your championship racket.

Eric Annihilated them all in me time.

Ernie Like who?

Eric The greatest ever.

Ernie Who was that?

Eric Only Lew Grade.

Ernie Lew Hoad.

Eric He's changed his name again to protect the innocent! Where's the barley water?

Ernie You don't need barley water, this is just a friendly game.

Eric I don't play friendly games. I'm known as the Killer of the Court.

Ernie I can see that I'm going to have quite a game.

Eric Just get down there and whip a few up. I'll take it easy to begin with.

Ernie You'll take it easy.

Eric I won't belt them back at you at the start, give you a chance to get used to my speed of return.

Ernie Shall I serve or will you?

Eric Fine.

Ernie I'll spin the racket. You call.

Eric Heads.

Ernie Heads?

Ernie spins Eric's racket: it falls on ground and breaks into pieces.

Ernie I'll serve.

Eric You've broken my racket.

Ernie Use this one. *(Hands Eric a racket)* It's a wonder to me that you've never played at Wimbledon.

Eric What's that got to do with tennis? Get down there and whip a few up.

Ernie Ready?

Eric Any time you like, sunshine.

Eric crouches waiting for Ernie's serve. After a couple of seconds the ball flashes past Eric.

Eric *(Still crouched)* You can whip one up as soon as you like.

Ernie appears at his side of the net, beckons to Eric. Eric goes up to net.

Ernie Fifteen love.

Eric What are you talking about, fifteen love? You've got to get one past me first.

Ernie I have got one past you. *(Points to ball at back of Eric's side of the court)* Fifteen love.

Eric *(Looks at the tennis ball)* That was there before, that was.

Ernie Fifteen love. *(With contempt)* Lew Grade. I'll serve a bouncy one.

Eric I don't like bouncy ones. You belt them as hard as you like.

Ernie Very well.

Ernie goes out of shot to his side of the court. Eric crouches, waiting.

Ernie Ready?

Eric I'm ready. This time you won't even see it when I belt it back. Just a white blur if you're lucky. *(Ern's serve flashes past Eric)* Any time you like and as hard as you like.

Ernie appears at his side of the net, beckons to Eric. Eric goes up to net.

Ernie Thirty love.

Eric Thirty love what?

Ernie Thirty love. Just belted another one past you, you didn't even move.

Eric I was talking, wasn't I?

Ernie You've never stopped talking since we came on to this court. You've never stopped boasting about how good you are.

Eric What chance do I stand when I'm playing against somebody who cheats?

Ernie Thirty love.

Eric *(Very determined)* Right then, matie. Forearm smash you'll get now.

Ernie You're good at the forearm smash then?

Eric Who do you think taught the forearm smash to Yvonne Dinnergong? I'll destroy you now, matie.

Ernie Thirty love.

Ernie goes off to his side of the court.

Ernie Ready?

Eric You'll find out how ready I am.

Eric crouches, waiting and swaying slightly from side to side. After long pause the ball flashes past him. Ernie appears at the net and beckons to Eric. Eric goes to net.

Ernie Forty love.

Eric What kind of a way do you call that to play tennis? Half an hour I was waiting for that ball.

Ernie Quite within the rules – serve in my own time and if you're not ready it's hardly my fault. Forty love.

Eric tries to contain his anger.

Ernie *(With contempt)* Yvonne Dinnergong!

Ernie goes to his side of the court.

Eric And stop walking like Virginia Wade to try and put me off!

Ernie Ready?

Eric Yes, I'm ...

Ball flashes past Eric, again he doesn't move. Ernie appears at net: beckons to Eric. Eric goes to net.

Ernie First game to me, I think, champ.

Eric How am I supposed to play tennis without barley water? Should be barley water here.

Ernie You must be worn out the way you've shot around this court. Nevertheless, first set to me.

Eric You'll get yours now it's my turn to serve. Machine Gun Morecambe.

Ernie Got a good serve then?

Eric It'll be so fast the draught from it will whip that right off your head.

Ernie I'll risk it.

Ernie goes to his side of the net.

Eric Ready for blastoff?

Ernie Whenever you like, champ.

Eric You won't even see this one, I promise you that.

Eric does a terrible serve: ball goes up and over the hedge.

Ernie *(Laughing loudly)* You're right, I didn't see it. Any more good serves like that one, champ? Where did you get those shorts: Rent-a-tent?

Eric looks really angry. He serves another terrible one and the ball again goes over hedge.

Ernie *(Laughing)* Love fifteen, champ. Keep going. I'll win this game without playing a stroke.

Eric prepares for an almighty serve: he throws the ball up, swings at it, misses it completely. He hurls his racket over the net. Loud cry from Ernie.

Eric Out like a light. Game, set and match to me.

Ernie My famous play about Napoleon next.

Eric With Vanessa Redcoat?

Ernie Redgrave. She gave us a few problems.

Eric With her being such a tall girl?

Ernie Do you know she wanted paying by the inch.

Eric We'd have been skint. A delightful lady to work with.

Ernie Affable.

Eric Always thought she was British.

Ernie She worked hard at rehearsal.

Eric Did you see her during the breaks? She was stretched out fast asleep in three separate dressing rooms.

Ernie Vanessa rather liked me.

Eric Oh?

Ernie Offered me a lift home in her car.

Eric Fool!

Ernie What do you mean?

Eric It was only because she didn't have a dipstick.

Ernie This is a play of mine we did in one of our Christmas shows with Vanessa Redgrave.

Eric We wanted a big bird for Christmas and we got one.

Vanessa Redgrave

There was one line in the Napoleon and Josephine sketch that I've always been particularly pleased with. It was inevitable that Eric would comment on Vanessa's gracious height. It came at the end of the dialogue in front of the curtains before 'Ern's Play' started.

Ernie I think you should go and get ready to appear in my play, Miss Vanessa.
Vanessa Of course. I'll be right back.
Eric You're big enough to play in goal.

This was also the occasion when I was told that I was 'out of order' by a cameraman for giving Eric an extra line to use on his first entrance. The cameraman was quite right to tick me off because all lines are rehearsed, are known to the cameraman and are cue-lines for his shots. There was a bronze eagle on a plinth, and I suggested that on his entrance Eric should stop, tap the metal bird and say 'You've been giving this bird too much millet'. Two of us thought it was funny.

Vanessa was a superb Josephine and a very fine dancer as she showed in the Latin dance routine. If you don't want to see Vanessa's Flamenco look away now.

Napoleon & Josephine

CAST IN ORDER OF HEIGHT

Empress Josephine – Vanessa Redgrave

Duke of Ellington – Eric Morecambe

Napoleon Bonaparte – Duke Ern of Peterborough

Lord Brighton – Brian Clough

Minister without Portfolio – Larry Grayson

Regimental Goat – Richard Attenborough

Horses trained by Mrs Mark Phillips
Cannon balls supplied by Fanny Craddock
The BBC wishes to thank the British Museum
for the uniforms and jokes.

Scene: in the richly furnished tent used by Napoleon on the battlefield of Waterloo. Tent is deserted. F/X heavy gunfire and the distant shouting of men in battle. Ernie enters as Napoleon: staggers around the tent before standing still and looking very distressed.

Ernie Sacre Beaujolais! That it should come to this – that I, Napoleon Bonaparte, the tenacious Corsican, should come to this. Defeated by that devil, Wellington. Sacre Beaujolais and bon appetit.

Ernie bows his head and is sobbing ... as Vanessa Redgrave enters as Josephine, looking seductive. She stops and sees Ernie sobbing.

Vanessa He is crying again. I wish he wouldn't cry. The tears roll down his legs and make them shrink. I do love him. When he kisses me I can feel his heart beating against my kneecaps.

She crosses to Ernie and places an arm on his shoulder.

Vanessa Napoleon, sit down.

Ernie I am sat down.

Vanessa Napoleon, my beloved, tell your Josephine what has happened.

Ernie The flower of the French Army lies crushed upon the battlefield of Waterloo. I have lost some of my finest men.

Vanessa What about the big red-headed drummer lad?

Ernie What?

Vanessa The one with the big cymbals.

Ernie Oh him. Gone. Your Napoleon has been defeated.

Vanessa You must have known in your heart that defeat was inevitable.

Ernie I must be honest, two nights ago I had a slight inkling.

Vanessa Why didn't you tell me? I was awake. I take it that you have lost to the Duke of Wellington.

Ernie He is at this very moment on his way here with the terms of the surrender.

Sound of horses' hooves. Eric enters as Wellington. Hooves continue.

Eric That horse never stops ... Evenin' all. Sorry I'm late. Some fool kept me talking. Said he wanted to name a rubber boot after me. The Duke of Wellington at your service.

Eric salutes. Ernie salutes; pulls rabbit out of jacket.

Ernie Napoleon Bonaparte.

Eric *(Walks past Vanessa to Ernie.)* I don't want to worry you but this tent pole's loose.

Ernie How dare you, sir. That tent pole is the Empress Josephine.

Ernie places a small box in front of Vanessa. He stands on it and faces her.

Ernie Tell him who you are.

Vanessa I am indeed the Empress Josephine of France.

Eric And what are you doing up at the front? Not that it matters – it suits you.

Vanessa The Emperor wishes to discuss the Battle of Waterloo.

Eric Odd name for a battle. There was no water and I couldn't find a ...

Ernie *(Getting off box)* How dare you!

Vanessa Boney, my darling.

Ernie Not tonight, Josephine.

Eric What does he mean?

Ernie It is of little consequence.

Vanessa *(Looking at Eric)* I'll second that.

Eric *(To standard)* What do you think of it so far – *(Vents)* 'Ruggish'.

Ernie Now let's sit down and discuss these terms properly.

Vanessa I'll take everything down.

Eric That'll get a few laughs.

Vanessa and Eric sit down.

Vanessa Have you got the scrolls?

Eric No, I always walk like this.

Ernie The meeting is now in session.

He bangs table with mallet: hits Eric's finger.

Eric Ow!

Vanessa *(Reads paper)* These terms are a bit one-sided.

Ernie I'll say they are. Are you prepared to ratify *my* proposals?

Eric Certainly. Put them on the table and pass me that mallet.

Vanessa You want everything your own way.

Eric Oh, you've heard!

Ernie We are having no part of this document.

Vanessa What happens when Napoleon signs these surrender terms?

Eric He will be dragged out by the dragoons. Not a pretty sight! *(To Vanessa)* I wouldn't look if I were you.

Vanessa I've never heard anything so terrible.

Eric Oh, you must have done! Have you heard Max Bygraves singing 'Deck of Cards' – that takes a bit of beating.

Ernie Perfectly true, duke.

Eric Anyway, you will be taken to St Helena and incarcerated.

Vanessa *That'll* bring tears to his eyes.

Eric *(To camera)* They're all at it.

Ernie I think I should have a word with you, Josephine. *(Stands.)* Over here. *(Points, and pulls rabbit out.)*

Vanessa and Ernie move to one side. Eric moves behind them and listens.

Ernie We've got to find a way out of this.

Vanessa He's such a stubborn man.

Ernie It's not going to be easy.

Vanessa We could offer him money.

Ernie I've got an idea.

Vanessa What's that?

Eric Seduce him.

Vanessa *(To Ernie)* Do you think I could?

Eric Yes. He'd love it.

Ernie That's a good idea.

Ernie turns to Eric.

Ernie My Lord Duke ...

Eric Oh, there you are. I didn't understand a word because you were talking in French. Are you talking in French now?

Ernie No, I'm not ... I need time to study these terms.

Vanessa *(Aside to Ernie)* Just give me five minutes alone with him.

Eric That's no good. It takes me twenty minutes to get my wellies off.

Ernie I shall be in the anteroom. *(Exits)*

Vanessa We are alone.

Eric Ready when you are, pally.

Vanessa Poor Napoleon, he's been going through a bad time. Since his retreat from Moscow, he's been very cold towards me.

Eric Well, with that deep snow and those short legs ... say no more. *(Nudges Vanessa)* Would um ... *(Moves centre, to bed)* ... would you like something to warm you up?

Vanessa I would very much.

Eric Good. I think I've got some extra-strong mints in my greatcoat.

Vanessa I think no. Wellie ...?

Eric Yes.

Vanessa Napoleon has been so engrossed in the battle that he's tended to neglect me.

Eric Oh.

Vanessa I am a woman.

Eric Have you told him?

Vanessa I like you. *(She sprays perfume on to her neck)* 'Midnight in Paris'.

Eric *(Picks up bottle and dabs his cheeks with it.)* Two fifteen in Darlington – just before the kick-off.

Vanessa indicates that Eric should sit on the sofa.

Vanessa Please?

Eric Do you want to sell it?

Vanessa Sit by me. I only wish we had some music.

Eric That's easily arranged.

Picks up hat: it turns into accordion.

Vanessa I am beginning to like you very much. I wish we could have met in Paris. It's a beautiful city. Put the candle out.

Eric Where's the switch?

Vanessa Blow it out and we can make love.

Eric Yes. *(Attempts to blow candle out, but it lights each time)* By the time I blow this thing out I'll be too tired to make love.

Vanessa Never mind the candle. *(She cuddles up to Eric)* The better the light, the better the love.

Eric It's no use, I've just had a power cut.

Vanessa I think I'm falling in love with you.

Eric I have a wife at home in England.

Vanessa It's common knowledge that your wife has another.

Eric Now there's a novelty.

Vanessa Kiss me.

Vanessa throws her arms about Eric. A very long kiss. Eric shudders and bangs his legs.

Eric Good lord. Have you got shares in Mothercare?

Vanessa I don't know what it is you're doing to me, but I can feel a pounding in my bosom.

Eric Have a look, it might be one of his rabbits.

Vanessa *(Sits up)* So you think you can resist me.

Eric lunges and misses.

Eric Oh yes.

Vanessa Really?

She raises her skirt and reveals a Luton Town rosette just below her knee.

Eric I've got news for you, we're going up the League.

Eric and Vanessa embrace and lean back. Ernie enters.

Ernie Sacre Beaujolais and bon appetit. What is going on?

Vanessa and Eric both quickly rise.

Vanessa Napoleon!

Eric Don't jump to conclusions. I can explain everything. I was carrying on with your wife behind your back.

Ernie This is too much.

Takes hand from tunic and brings out rabbit.

Eric Have you got Harry Corbett in there passing them up to you?

Ernie First I lose a battle. Now I have lost my wife.

Vanessa That's not true.

Ernie I love you so much, Josephine. You must choose between me or him.

Eric *(Pulls his hand out – no rabbit.)* Yes, you must choose between me or him. And remember, this is the book of the play and we can't finish with a song.

Vanessa What a shame because I thought I sang so well.

Eric I couldn't hear you. You were too high up.

Ernie Josephine, the time has come for you to choose.

Eric I know we finished the sketch with a song on the telly but this is the book so think of a new tag or we're all in trouble.

Vanessa Very well.

Ernie You have made your choice, Josephine?

Vanessa I have.

Ernie Is it me?

Vanessa No.

Eric Then it is me!

Vanessa No.

Eric If it's not me ...

Ernie And it's not me ...

Vanessa It is Christmas and with the money you're paying me I won't have a decent dinner so I'll take the rabbit.

She reaches inside Eric's tunic and takes the rabbit.

Eric Don't go. I've got twelve more rabbits hidden away in there if you'd care to get them out.

Vanessa Gladly.

She puts her hand inside Eric's tunic.

Eric Oh yes! Keep going.

Arise Dame Ernie

Ernie Wise, OBE. These three proud initials stand for, according to Eric, Owns Banks Everywhere. He said it when the three of us were sitting in Eric's dressing room during a rehearsal break. This was quite usual. When I went to the recording we took every opportunity to throw ideas around to see how each would react.

The idea for an opening spot based on Ernie being mentioned in the honours list was pounced on instantly. I'd just suggested the OBE gag and the knighthood idea was a natural follow-up to this. The routine seemed to be loaded with humour because amongst other things it would allow us to play on Ern's pomposity when Eric told him he was to be made a lord. He was only going to be 'sir', but there was enough in the BBC budget to make him a 'lord'.

The wonderful thing about giving words to a gifted comedian is that he can make them so much better, far funnier than they look on paper. 'Her Majesty' said as it is written is not funny, but when Eric said those words in a high-pitched voice and pronounced them as 'Her Majest-ee' it was instant comic irreverence and very funny.

This opening spot was, as far as I was concerned, one of the best that Ernie ever did. In this we saw a master-class performance in the art of comedy timing and expression. He knew all the time that he was being conned by Eric, but never got angry or upset at the insults because it was just, just possible that he might be 'Lord Ern of Peterborough'. Was Ern made a lord? If you don't want to know the answer, look away now, or whistle 'Moonlight Serenade' up the leg of your kilt.

Ernie We've know each other for over thirty-four years and during that time I would say that we've been friends for at least twenty minutes.

Eric I take it then that you haven't read the *Harpenden Bugle and Advertiser*? Stop press.

Quickly looks at the newspaper, puts it away quickly ... whistling.

Ernie There is something about me in that newspaper?

Eric A chair for Mr Wise, please.

Curtains open: we see throne.

Ernie *(Looking at throne)* For me?

Eric Please, Ern.

He indicates throne.

Ernie Gosh!

Ernie sits on throne.

Eric Sit down.

Ernie I am sat down. Read what it says about me in that paper.

Eric *(Takes out newspaper)* I was close to tears when I read this. *(Looks at paper as though to read it, then lowers it)* Ern, you've come a long way since those early days when you played the part of 'Boy' and 'Cheetah' in those Tarzan pictures.

Ernie I wish you wouldn't mention that.

Eric *(Looking at paper)* Ern, try not to get too excited as I read out ... The New Year's Honours List!

Makes a trumpet noise.

Ernie New Year's Honours List!

Eric Sit down.

Ernie I am sat down. Read the New Year's Honours List.

Eric *(Reads from newspaper)* Her Most Gracious Majesty ...

Ernie Gosh!

Eric Her Most Gracious Majesty is pleased to bestow the following titles upon the undernamed. To John Betjeman – a sirhood.

Ernie He's been a 'sir' for years.

Eric For that poem he wrote.

There was a young lady from Preston
Who ran down the M1 with no vest on.
She was just outside Stoke
When this big hairy bloke
Said I've never seen one with a crest on.

Ernie He never wrote that.

Eric He did on a Christmas card. It was never published.

Ernie What does it say about me?

Eric Her Most Gracious Majesty bestows upon Ernie Wise – short-legged comedian

– the title of Lord – Lord Ern of Peterborough.

Ernie leaps to his feet.

Ernie Lord Ern of Peterborough!

Eric goes down on his knees.

Eric And now, Ern, you're the shortest knight of the year. *(Reads from paper)* It says here, in brackets, 'For services to literature'.

Ernie I've got it for those plays what I wrote. Let me see it.

Eric *(Hands paper to Ern)* It's in the stop press.

Ernie looks at newspaper: Eric is seated on the throne.

Ernie Gosh! *(Looks at Eric)* You're in my chair. *(Hits him with paper).*

Eric *(Rises)* I crave pardon, my lord.

Ernie *(Sits on throne)* Lord Ern of Peterborough. That means that my wife is now a lady.

Eric Give you something to do during the long winter nights.

Ernie I will have to kneel before the Queen.

Eric She'll never reach you with a sword.

Ernie I'll have to move to a big posh house. Tea on the lawn, eating croquet.

Eric You'll like them. Especially the well-done ones.

Ernie Cowes over the weekend.

Eric You dirty little devil. Of course, you realise you'll need a monogram.

Ernie I'll have no time for playing records.

Eric That's true.

Ernie I'll buy my mother a new home.

Eric Nothing wrong with the one you bought her last year. Plenty of room if the dog moves over a bit.

Ernie I can't live in the flat now.

Eric Now you're being selfish. Who's the cat going to play with if you go?

Ernie I suppose my wife will want a daily.

Eric You'll have to get a sailor in, then.

Ernie It won't be easy for you but I'm sure you'll get by without me.

Eric Never, my lord. Could Popeye get by without Olive Oil? Losing you, it's like ... it's like losing my little finger. I crave compassion for a commoner, my lord!

Ernie Touch your forelock – oh no, you can't. You haven't got a forelock.

Eric You rotten devil.

Ernie Who's narked because he isn't mentioned in the Honours List? *(Stands behind Eric)* Who's narked because he isn't mentioned in the Honours List. Who's a bit jealous then?

Eric *(Turns)* Shut your face.

Ernie Shut your face, *my lord. (Offers Eric his hand)* Well, I must be going now. It's been topping knowing you, Morecambe.

Both shake hands.

Eric In spite of everything I wish you a happy Christmas, my lord.

Ernie As I do. I hope you get a lot of fun out of the little gift I bestowed on you.

Eric A lovely little typewriter, my lord, even if it was second hand.

Ernie It works, doesn't it?

Eric I have tried it out and it does work – you can see for yourself here in the stop press column of the *Harpenden Bugle and Advertiser.*

Shows Ernie the paper.

Ernie Yes, it works beautifully. *(Realises)* You typed out this New Year's Honours List!!

They argue loudly as they exit.

The Calculator Sketch

This sketch was set in a shop, a favourite situation in many of the shows. This piece was written just a few days after I had purchased the very item Eric wants from Ernie's shop.

Shop doorbell as door opens and Eric enters. Ernie is behind the counter.

Ernie Can I help you?

Eric Is this shop open?

Ernie It says 'Open' on the sign hanging on the door.

Eric It says 'Closed'.

Ernie It says 'Open' from the outside.

Pause while Eric works this out.

Eric That's clever.

Ernie Can I help you?

Eric Calculator.

Ernie We are specialists.

Eric Then I need go no further.

Ernie Rest assured.

Eric I don't want a mattress.

Ernie We know all there is to know about calculators. We have been selling electronic equipment for over five hundred years. If I may show you a selection of our calculators?

Places selection of calculators on counter.

Eric Thank you. Do they vary in price or do they cost different amounts?

Ernie Well, they vary in price but some do cost different amounts.

Eric I see.

Ernie You require a calculator for your work?

Eric British High Commissioner to the Bahamas.

Ernie That's a very important post.

Eric Had I have got the job it would have been. I'm a plumber's mate. When I say I'm

his mate, that means I just help him with his work and that's as far as it goes.

Ernie I understand.

Eric May I try one of your calculators?

Ernie That calculator will work out anything.

Eric Let me see now. *(As he speaks he uses the calculator)* Married fifteen years ... fifty-two weeks in the year ... fifty-two multiplied by fifteen equals ... seven hundred and eighty weeks. Now multiply seven hundred and eighty by four ... three thousand one hundred and twenty. That is amazing.

Ernie Three thousand one hundred and twenty what, sir?

Eric It's got nothing to do with you. I'll buy that when I've had a sit-down.

Summer Night in the Garden

Another of my favourite pieces took place in the garden on a very warm summer afternoon. Ernie was relaxing in a chair and listening to 'Summer Night on the River'. I wanted this sketch to be played slow to create the sort of languid and lazy mood of a summer afternoon. To my surprise they both played this scene even slower than I had suggested and it worked.

We heard the music and saw Ernie relaxing for quite a while before Eric entered. It was John Ammonds' idea to hold the opening shot for so long and it was a good one.

Eric Lovely day for it, Ern.

Ernie Lovely day for it?

Eric If you like.

Ernie No jokes. *(Pause.)* It's hot.

Eric It's the heat.

Ernie Take a chair.

Eric I've got one at home.

Just sit down.

Eric I'd rather stand. *(He sits down)* Garden looks nice.

Ernie Good.

Eric I like those red flowers, the geronimos.

Ernie Geraniums. *(Pause)* It's hot.

Eric It's the heat. Nice music.

Ernie Delius.

Eric Is he British?

Ernie Bradford.

Eric Could have sworn he was British *(Pause, then looks up pointing)* Woodpecker.

Ernie Woodpecker?

Eric Just flown out of that tree.

Ernie How do you know it was a woodpecker?

Eric I could smell the cider. *(Chuckles.)*

Ernie Please.

Pause.

Eric What do they call of those little tiny insects with lots of legs?

Ernie Don't know and I don't care.

Eric You should.

Ernie Why?

Eric One of them's just crawled up the leg of your shorts.

Ernie *(Leaps to his feet.)* What!!

Eric *(Laughing.)* That's what's known as a journey into the unknown.

Percy Thrower

In the 1970s Percy Thrower ruled supreme as the number one gardening expert on television, Delia Smith with a spade. When Percy arrived on the first morning of rehearsal he was carrying a small holdall. Eric said, 'I'd heard that you were a perfectionist, Percy, but you didn't have to bring your own manure'. Eric, like myself, was not all that keen on gardening; the only thing that either of us could grow was tired.

There was one gag in the Percy Thrower sketch that I liked very much but it was taken out on the grounds that it was more suited to radio. I'm determined not to waste it, so here it is. Eric told Ernie that he had grown rhubarb twenty feet high. An astonished Ernie asked him how he did this and the answer came when Frankie Lane was heard singing just this one line 'Champion the wonder horse'.

My horticultural ignorance was exposed when I named some of the blooms to be used in the sketch as 'nifferaniums and happydown dilldocks'. It was left to Percy to give them something more acceptable to gardening enthusiasts.

Ernie liked the idea of working with Percy, as he was very keen on gardening and horticulture in general. He claimed that he used to listen to *The Archers* when they only had a window box. That was another line in the sketch that never made it to the screen.

Percy showed Eric some very large potatoes and told him that they were King Edwards. Eric looked at them and said 'They're more like King Kong's.' You are now invited to turn the page and join Percy Thrower and friends in the greenhouse, as they press their bulbs into the warm earth ...

I wouldn't have got away with that one either in 1970.

Gardener's Wild

Ernie Good evening. My name is Ernest Wheatsheaf and my speciality is growing roses. This one for instance. *(Points to chrysanthemum)* This is one of my champion roses. We are today in Percy Thrower's garden. He should be here at any moment. Here he comes now.

Percy enters

Ernie Hello, Percy, and thank you for inviting me down to see your plants.

Percy It's nice to see you here, Mr Wheatsheaf.

Ernie There's a lot of work here for one man, Percy.

Percy There is but I've just engaged a new assistant. He should be here somewhere. Ah, here he comes now.

Eric enters.

Eric Evenin' all. Sorry I'm late, only I've been bedding out and the wife caught me.

Ernie Hello.

Percy This is Adam.

Ernie Adam?

Eric Adam Pruned.

Ernie Nice to meet you, Adam. My name's Ernest Wheatsheaf.

Eric Ah, I've seen you on the television. There's only three programmes I watch. Mr Thrower here, Fanny Craddock and the television doctor ... Percy grows 'em, Fanny cooks 'em and the doctor shows us how to get better.

Ernie *(Laughs)* A good rural joke! We are on television at the moment. *(Eric stares at camera)* Percy, these plants must be very difficult to grow. Can you tell me something about them?

Percy Certainly. Now that flower over there is very unusual. It's a *Kniphofia uvaria.* Would you pass it over please, Adam?

Eric grabs the plant and it snaps off at the stem ... There is a stunned silence.

Ernie These look very interesting over here, Percy.

Percy Ah yes, that's a variety of *Noble secundus.* I've had those now for some five years and taken very great care of them. They thrive on being sprayed. *(Eric sprays a plant)* But never in daylight. *(Flowers fall off)*

Ernie Of course, only a fool would spray in daylight. Shall we move on? What's that long, tall thing?

Eric That's my wife.

Ernie It looks like a rubber plant.

Percy Over there we have a very interesting variety of rubber plant.

Ernie I've heard that these have got to be pruned to perfection.

Percy Oh yes. Everything depends on the pruning. You see that there? *(Points to point near base. Eric cuts the plant)*

Ernie What's so special about that?

Percy Never prune them there.

Ernie *(To Adam)* Never. I see. Will you make a note of that Adam?

Eric Yes. Never prune them there.

Ernie Do you suffer with many pests in this garden?

Percy Only this one. *(Looks at Eric)*

Ernie *(Laughs)* Another rural joke! Do you grow some of these? *(Picks up seeds)*

Percy Oh, be very careful with those. *(Takes them from Ernie. Pours them into his hand)* The few that you see here in my hand are the only ones in the world.

Eric sneezes and all the seeds are blown out of Ernie's hand.

Ernie Shall we move on? What is your most prized possession, Percy?

Percy This is the most prized possession in my garden. *Mexicanus Delicti* - a very special flower.

Ernie But what's so special about it?

Percy Well it only blooms once every forty years and by pure coincidence it so happens that this is the time it's due to bloom. Literally any second now.

Ernie Well why don't we take a picture of it? *(Takes camera from shoulder)*

Eric It's moving now.

Plant starts to move. Eric stands in front of the plant. He obscures Ernie's and Percy's view. Ernie takes picture of back of Eric's hand.

Eric Did you get it, did you get the picture? Better luck next time, Percy.

Ernie Percy, what's that queer-looking object over there?

Percy That's my wife.

Ernie It's all droopy.

Eric That's my wife.

Percy Ah, that is a most unusual plant that only just arrived from South America. It's the pitcher plant. It traps insects. A very rare flower with a most unusual perfume.

Eric I'll get it Perce.

Percy Will you excuse me a minute?

Ernie Certainly Percy.

Percy I'm going next door for a dibber.

Eric Well have one for me while you're there.

Ernie Before you go, Percy, can you tell me some more about this plant with the unusual perfume? Could I smell it?

Percy No, whatever you do don't smell it.

Ernie What would happen, Percy?

Eric meanwhile has smelled the flower. It has stuck to his nose and he is trying to get it off.

Percy Well, if you were to smell it, it would stick to your nose and then five minutes later it would eat your nose completely.

Eric *(To Ernie)* Could I have a word with you please?

Percy Quick, get it off.

Fade as all struggle to free Eric.

Old Man Sketch

Boys enter: Eric is on a walking stick, wearing a white alpaca jacket and a white straw hat. He is made up to look very old with grey hair sticking out from under the hat.

Ernie Good evening, ladies and gentlemen – welcome to the show.

Eric Tell me what you think.

Ernie What do you mean? What do I think?

Eric Me! Look at me.

Ernie *(Looking)* Very smart, just as smart and as well turned out as you are every week.

Eric Smart?

Ernie As always. Tonight we thought that ...

Eric No, Ern. That make-up, the grey hair, the wrinkles. I asked them to make me look like a very old man.

Ernie Do you know I didn't notice the difference. *(Laughs)* I really didn't notice the difference.

Eric But they've been very nearly four hours making me look like this.

Ernie If they'd have waited another month or so they wouldn't have had to bother. *(Laughs)*

Eric looks hurt.

Eric I'm supposed to be a very old man not quite in possession of his factories.

Ernie Faculties!

Eric Just a moment. Can he say faculties? *(Pause)* They're checking up. *(Pause)* No – faculties. Yes, you can.

Ernie All right! You want me to ask why you are you dressed like an old man.

Eric Who?

Ernie You.

Eric Yes. I have just been offered a character part in a film.

Ernie And what am I supposed to do?

Eric How many plays have you written?

Ernie Oh, Lord knows.

Eric That's probably true but He can't have seen every one.

Ernie What have my plays got to do with it?

Eric You've written lots of character parts and I thought you might be able to give me a few ideas about how to play the part of an old man.

Ernie But what about my audience.

Eric He rang earlier – he's gone to bingo.

Ernie Oh, all right. I'll help you. That's what friends are for. Now show me your old man's walk.

Eric Certainly. *(Walks upstage)* Are you ready?

Ernie Yes.

Eric One old man's walk coming up.

Eric walks briskly downstage.

Ernie No idea! You look like Lionel Blair.

Eric Well, he is getting on a bit.

Ernie Give me that stick and I'll show you.

Ernie walks down as old man.

Eric That was marvellous. Now can you talk like an old man because I find that very difficult.

Ernie walks upstage, then down.

Ernie *(Old voice)* Hello, young fellow me lad, I'm an old man.

Eric looks right and left.

Eric Keep those sheep out of here.

Ernie *(Very proud)* It was me.

Eric Good Lord. Do it again!

Ernie *(Old voice)* Hello, young fellow me lad, I'm an old man.

Eric Ladies and gentlemen. An Oscar winner on a stick.

Ernie Now watch this bit now ... *(Knees shaking)* My knees, they're trembling.

Eric It's a few years since that happened, but I won't ask you to do the next bit because it's too difficult even for you. Thanks anyway, Ern, let's go now and ...

Ernie Too difficult for me? Name it.

Eric Not even you, Ern.

Ernie Name it!

Eric Well, in the film this very old man, he dies.

Ernie That's easy!

He walks upstage.

Eric Are you doing it now?

Ernie No! *(He staggers for dying act)* Ahh! Ooh! Ahhh!

Eric *(Watching Ernie)* Good Lord! That is astounding, that is.

Ern makes the most of the dying act, and finishes up on floor. Gets up and 'dies' again on floor.

Eric Thank you very much Ern. That's perfect for the film, because it has be a very, very, old man.

Ernie What's the film called?

Eric The Ernie Wise story. *(To camera)* He'll never learn.

The Health Food Shop

Ernie was the inspirational spark that brought this sketch to life. He was one of the fittest men I have ever worked with, as fit as a boarding-house flea. He was a good tennis player, a very strong swimmer, played a lot of cricket and he really did love sailing his boat. I wonder if he ever found out that in his absence we referred to him as 'Popeye'?

Eric's favourite outdoor hobby was one we both shared: birdwatching. One morning we both went o'er bush and heath, Eric raised his binoculars very quickly and said 'Write this down quick!' I really was excited: 'What is it?' He replied, 'A great big pole tied down with two thick wires.' Needless to say that before the expedition was over Eric had also sighted Percy Thrower with a suitcase strapped to his legs flying south for the winter. He also saw a kestrel. When in my surprise I said, 'Good Lord,' Eric said, 'No, I can't see him.'

During a conversation with Ernie on the merits of healthy foods he asked me what it was that helped me to relax. I told him 'Delius'. Ern looked rather puzzled then asked, 'Is that powder or liquid?' How could I not write a health food sketch?

Eric is seated alone in the flat watching television: from the TV set we hear fanfare and voice of Hughie Green.

Voice And now friends it's 'Make your mind up time'.

Eric I have ... *(Quickly switches off and rises)* It's obvious who's going to win it this week – it'll be that eighty-eight-year-old lady from Cheltenham playing 'Sonny Boy' on the watering can. If she doesn't it'll be the Chelsea Pensioner who did the splits over the live lobster. I don't know where he gets them from. I wish Ernie would hurry up at the supermarket. I'm starving. I wouldn't mind betting that he's met that fellow doing the soap commercial for the television, offering Ern two big ones for his little one – he won't swap. He's a good lad, Ernie, he's gone out for those groceries without a murmur – I don't know what I'd do without him ... buy a hamster probably.

Door to flat is kicked from the outside. Ernie cannot open the door as he has his hands full of groceries: he calls out.

Ernie Are you in there, Eric!!

Eric I don't know. I'll have to look. *(Looks inside jacket)* Yes, I am!

Ernie Come on, open up!

Eric moves towards the door and opens it: Ernie staggers in under the weight of a large cardboard box full of groceries.

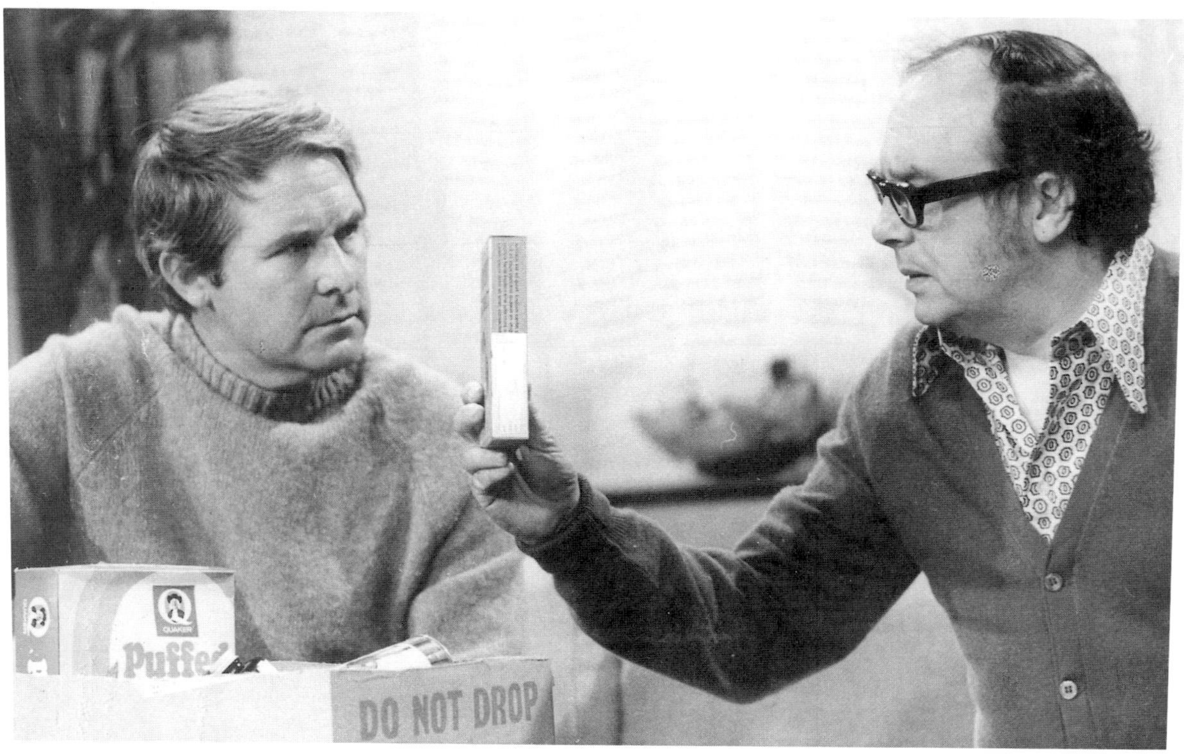

Ernie This lot's heavy.

Eric Did you get the groceries?

Ernie Give me a hand.

Eric You shouldn't be carrying heavy things like that, you'll displace it again.

Ernie Don't just stand there. *(Puts box on settee)*

Eric What took you so long?

Ernie I met that fellow who offered me two big ones for my little one.

Eric You didn't swap, did you?

Ernie No, I didn't.

Eric I knew you wouldn't. Come on.

Eric helps Ernie to lower the box.

Ernie Any telephone calls for me while I was out?

Eric A director rang from Hollywood. Alfred somebody.

Ernie Hitchcock?

Eric He might have, I didn't ask.

Ernie He wants a thriller from me.

Eric Some hopes ... What have you got, I'm starving.

Ernie Plenty here.

Eric Good lad. *(Looks into box ... takes out packet)* That's all I needed.

Ernie What's wrong?

Eric You've been there again, haven't you?

Ernie Been where?

Eric That flaming health-food shop. That's the fourth time this week. I hate health foods. I'm up to here with wheat germ: if I go out I blow away in the breeze. And if I eat another starch-reduced roll and turn over in bed I'll crack.

Ernie Do you good this stuff will. You can't beat Mother Nature. Health foods build you up and make you strong. Give us a hand with this table.

Moves table in front of settee. They sit on settee.

Eric *(Looks at tin from box)* Sugarapsa! What's Sugarapsa?

Ernie *(Turns tin right way up)* Asparagus.

Eric I can't eat this muck.

Ernie It's not muck.

Eric I want proper food inside me.

Ernie This is proper food. *(Holds up jar of honey)* Look, honey, nature's miracle food.

Eric *(Takes jar and reads label)* 'Golden honey. Recalls the music of waves beating against the sun-drenched shores of the Caribbean.'

Ernie Yes.

Eric 'Bottled in Huddersfield.' You shouldn't eat honey.

Ernie Why not?

Eric A friend of mine, only twenty-six, got killed through honey.

Ernie Got killed through eating honey?

Eric Yes, a crate fell on his head. Take that rubbish back to the shop and get a couple of thick steaks and a few pounds of sausages. I've got to keep me strength up.

Eric We eat far too much these days. We only need fourteen hundred calories to stay healthy and I'm going to keep fit with nature foods and plenty of exercise. *(He gets up)*

Eric Right, I'll fetch your lead.

Ernie exercises.

Eric Don't overdo it, will you.

Ernie You don't seem to realise that the human body is like a factory.

Eric Oh. Are you on short time? Is the delicatessen shop still open?

Ernie And a lot of good the stuff they sell will do you.

Eric Mouthwatering some of the things they have hanging from the ceiling in that shop. I'm never sure whether it's food or somebody coming through the roof.

Ernie Not for me. I once had some snails from there.

Eric Took you six weeks to get to the bathroom. I might nip out to Wimpy's.

Ernie What for?

Eric A plate of Wimps.

Ernie Why don't you give this health food a try? You might even like it.

Eric *(Holding up a packet)* Puffed wheat – what are you trying to do to me? When I think of some of those meals we used to have at home when I was a lad. On a Sunday we'd have a roast duck – if the park was open.

Ernie *(Getting up)* Revolting that is.

Eric I take it then that you're deadly serious about nature and good health?

Ernie Never more so.

Eric Sit down and take the weight off your lavender bags.

Ernie sits on settee.

Ernie Well?

Eric You're serious about keeping healthy nature's way?

Ernie I've told you I am.

Eric Go the whole hog – join a nudist camp.

Ernie Me become a nudist?

Eric They'd let you join at a reduced price.

Ernie No, I couldn't go around with no clothes on.

Eric Well, take your cap in case you go shopping.

Ernie I couldn't become a nudist and that's final.

Eric *(Getting up)* Well, then that proves that you're only half-hearted about this whole nature business.

Goes to put coat on.

Ernie Where are you going?

Eric We're both going to take this lot back to the health shop, get our money back and buy some proper food.

Eric and Ernie enter the health food shop, carrying the cardboard box.

Ernie Put the box down. *(Both lower box)* I'll show you, I'll show you just how good health foods are for you. *(Looking round)* There's nobody about.

Eric They're all dead. You make me laugh the way you get these crazes every so often. Last week it was 'Men's Lib' and you set fire to your braces.

Ernie Say what you like. I'm going to keep myself in good trim.

Eric You sound like a wick. There's one of those keep-fit bikes.

Eric climbs on to bike and pedals.

Ernie Just you get off that bike.

Eric Saddle's a bit small. Put the colour back in my cheeks.

Eric gets off bike.

Ernie The man will be here in a minute.

Man appears behind the counter.

Man I'm sorry to have kept you I ...

Eric *(From bike)* Can you tell me the way to Aberdeen?

Moves to counter.

Man Hello, Mr Wise.

Ernie Hello, Mr Warmsley.

Man Back for more of our health-giving products?

Ernie One has to look after oneself, Mr Warmsley.

Man Indeed. Early to bed, early to rise ...

Eric Makes you a miser just like Ernie Wise. A quarter of gumdrops and two tins of blacin' please. And we'd like our money back for this rubbish that you sold my friend.

Ernie Mr Warmsley, I'd like you to meet my friend.

Man Your friend. I see.

Ernie I'm afraid that he doesn't believe in the health-giving properties of nature foods.

Man My dear fellow. You must read some of our literature.

Eric Got any nudists' books?

Man We don't stock that sort of thing. This might enlighten you as to our products.

Hands Eric a leaflet.

Eric *(Looks at leaflet)* What does this say?

Man *(Looks at leaflet)* Get rid of acne.

Eric That's not nice – my auntie lives there.

Ernie Excuse me. *(Crosses Eric)* You'll have a job trying to convince him, Mr Warmsley.

Man We can but try, Mr erm ...

Eric McQueen, Steve McQueen.

Man Well, Mr McQueen.

Eric You can call me Steve. I'm half a star.

Ernie Excuse me. *(Crosses)* Mr Warmsley is a wonderful advertisement for health foods. Tell him, Mr Warmsley.

Eric Yes, tell me, Mr Warmsley.

Man I've been on health foods for over twenty years now. Let me tell you something.

Eric Yes.

Man Many years ago
before reading about nature's foods I was always a little queer.

Eric There's no answer to that.

Ernie Tell him what the specialist said, Mr Warmsley.

Eric Yes, tell me what the specialist said, Mr Warmsley.

Man I was for ever feeling unwell and off-colour, no energy, listless.

Eric And?

Man I placed myself in the hands of a health food specialist. The first thing he did was to cut off my carbohydrates.

Eric *(Grabs him)* Just watch it. This is a family show!

Man I've got orders to prepare for genuine clients. I'll send somebody else out to attend to you. *(Exits)*

Eric Are we going to buy some real food now?

Ernie No, I'm still convinced that health foods are best.

Eric Suit yourself. *(Sees vibrator)* What's this contraption?

Ernie Helps you lose weight.

Eric *(Puts the belt around waist)* Have I lost any?

Ernie Switch it on. *(Switches belt on)*

Eric Oooh! By golly it doesn't half go ... me kneecaps are working loose ... me jockey shorts are up around me neck ... switch it off!!

Ernie *(Switches it off)* What do you think?

Eric I'll tell you something. I'm frightened to stamp me foot.

Ernie I wonder where Mr Warmsley's got to?

Girl enters behind counter.

Girl Can I help you?

Eric Good Lord, Mr Warmsley, that was a quick change.

Girl Hello, Mr Wise. I've got your tablets.

Hands bottle to Ernie.

Ernie Thank you.

Eric *(Takes tablets)* Hello, what are these for? Give me those. *(Looks at label)* Nurse Lusty's Virility Tablets?

Ernie Yes, they're mine. *(To girl)* Do I take them before or after?

Eric Instead of. For a Plentitude of Power? Fortifies the over-forties, Fractures the over-fifties. Puts you in fine fettle for it? Puts you in fine fettle for what?

Ernie Give me those tablets.

Eric Did you get these for him?

Girl Mr Wise did order them.

Eric You dirty little devil. No wonder you've been getting hot flushes. They're from Northern Spain – they give these to stallions. He's not having these, I'm responsible for him.

Ernie I'm over-age.

Eric But undersized. Two of these and you'd disappear completely. They could be dangerous.

Girl They've done my husband a power of good.

Eric Husband?

Girl Cyril. Twenty-five years of age and no energy at all till he tried those tablets.

Ernie He's been taking them, has he? *(Moves to the door)* By the way, how are the children?

Girl The quads are doing very well and the triplets start school next month.

A very jaded old man appears in the door leaning on a walking stick.

Man Hello, my dear.

Eric Is this your father?

Girl No, Cyril, my husband.

Eric Cyril? *(To Ernie)* Quick, I'm taking you home.

They exit.

John Mills

As soon as John Ammonds knew who the guest was going to be on the next show he would telephone me within minutes. Time was a luxury I could ill afford as I was never at any time a show in hand. For the next show we had landed a really big one, John Mills, and it didn't take long to dream up an idea – it had to be a prisoner of war sketch. *Colditz* had been very successful on BBC TV, as had John Mills in the film, but what to do in the three-way dialogue in front of the curtains before the sketch? For me, it was a dream because for the very first and only time in my career I could base that always tricky spot on something that had actually happened to me in real life.

I have never told this story before. It was long before I became a writer and I was trying to earn a living selling fruit and veg in Liverpool's St John's Market. St John's? Another coincidence. One Tuesday afternoon I was stacking oranges when a very cultured voice said, 'Excuse me, how much are these?' When I turned to face the potential customer I was unable to speak for a few seconds because I was staring with mouth open at John Mills and Joan Greenwood. Both were starring in a play at the Royal Court Theatre just across the road. It just didn't seem real. John Mills was standing just a couple of feet from me, an international film star holding two apples and asking how much they cost.

He paid me for the apples and gave one to Joan Greenwood. She gave me a lovely smile, John said 'Thank you' and they both turned to leave. 'Could I have your autographs please?' They said I could but the problem was I didn't have an autograph book. I fumbled around red-faced with embarrassment. When I asked 'Would er – would you mind signing this?' these two very kind, very understanding people wrote their names on a brown paper bag and handed it to me with a warm smile.

Sixteen years later John and I met at the BBC during rehearsal for 'Escape from Stalag 54' and very much to my astonishment he remembered that incident.

The opening in front of the curtains was almost a re-run of what actually happened, with one slight alteration: instead of a brown paper bag John Mills gave Eric his autograph on a banana.

Eric and Ernie are in front of tabs.

Eric Ladies and gentlemen, we would like you to meet a very fine actor. *(To Ernie)* It's not him.

Ernie When I was told that the man you're about to meet was free to appear in one of my plays I immediately cancelled my lecture tour of America. You'll understand why I was so pleased when I tell you that our guest tonight ...

Eric I wonder if he'll remember me?

Ernie You know him?

Eric Met him a long time ago. Play your cards right and you'll get him for nothing.

Ernie All the other guests we've had have done it for nothing.

Eric He'll do it for half of that. I wonder if he'll recognise me.

Ernie Let's find out. Ladies and gentlemen – Mr John Mills.

Applause as John enters.

Ernie Mr Mills, John, this is a very proud moment for me.

Eric is in background smiling and waiting to be recognised.

John And for me, Ernie. I've always wanted to be in one of your plays and I am delighted to see that you've written a prisoner of war play.

Ernie The action does take place in a prisoner of war camp in Germany which is just outside Berlin.

Eric Hello!

John That's a part I've played before. Remember *The Colditz Story*?

Ernie No.

John That's funny. It was quite a success. I played the senior escape officer.

Eric Did you get killed in the end?

John No.

Eric You will in this. If the Germans don't get you, the audience will.

John It's such a good subject, Mr Wise, full of tension and atmosphere.

Ernie It's a real nail-biter.

Eric *(Waves hands)* Hello.

John I think this chap is trying to attract your attention.

Ernie I don't think it's me he wants.

Eric You remember me?

John No. Now, about the play, Mr Wise ...

Eric One moment, sir. Cast your mind back to Manchester. Manchester 1952 – you were appearing in a play.

John I did appear in a play in Manchester in 1952.

Eric And a very find play it was too, sir, written by a great personal friend, W Somerset Morgan.

John No it was written by my wife, Mary Hayley Bell. I'm afraid I don't remember you and my wife doesn't remember you.

Ernie He doesn't know you, go and get ready.

Eric A small grocer's shop next door to the theatre, you came in one day and I asked you for your autograph – you signed it for me on a banana.

Ernie On a banana?

John I remember that.

Ernie You'd never forget autographing a banana.

John Eric!

Eric Yes. On that banana it said 'To Eric, Yours sincerely, John Fyffe Mills'.

John I remember that very well – it was a good few years ago.

Eric I've still got that banana!

John After all these years?

Eric I ate the banana but kept the skin. It's all shrivelled up now.

John It would be.

Eric Happens to us all in time. On that banana all you can read now is 'Jimills'.

Ernie Jimills?

Eric Ern, what do I say to you every time I see a banana?

Ernie John Mills.

Eric Sometimes I say to him, 'Don't just stand there, Ern, peel me a John Mills.'

John I see. I'd like to have a look at it some time.

Eric Hello! Another of 'em.

Ernie Anyway it's a great honour having your name in one of my shows.

Eric Mills – go like a bomb.

John I was dreading that.

Eric Weren't we all!

John Will, erm ... will you be appearing in this play, Eric?

Eric Yes, have no fear.

Ernie Mr Mills won an Oscar for acting.

Eric You're in good company here, son.

John You haven't won an Oscar, have you?

Eric A Percy.

John A Percy?

Ernie I've never heard of a Percy.

Eric Not quite as well known as an Oscar but not many people have won a Percy.

John What did you get the Percy for?

Eric Bird impressions.

John Bird impressions?

Eric You'd like to hear a few dozen now?

Ernie No!

Eric How about the mating call of the Gruffy bird? Most unusual little bird – got three legs and a squint – attracts its mate by rubbing its back legs together and setting fire to its saddlebag.

John Shall I go and get ready?

Ernie If you wouldn't mind because we have got a play to do.

John This is an escape play?

Ernie That's right.

John I think I'll make a break for it now.

Turns to go.

Eric What a lovely little mover. You know, it's rather nice. We've had your daughter on the show. And now we've got you and on the same show we've even got your mother.

John My mother?

Eric Yes, Mrs Mills – on the Joanna.

John exits.

Ernie *(To Eric)* One of these days you're going to say something sensible. Ladies and gentlemen, starring Ernest Wise and in a supporting role, John Mills, in a play about three British officers and their attempt to escape from a German prisoner of war camp called ... Escape from Stalag 54.

Eric He looks very much like his mother, doesn't he?

Ernie Why don't you shut up?

Cast in order of bank balance

Captain Hammond	Ernie Wise
Major Faversham	John Mills
Lieutenant D'Arcy	Eric Morecambe
Lillie Marlene	Mick Jagger
Camp Commandant	Sir Billy Butlin
Camp Guard Dog	Dougal
Camp Cook	Lionel Blair
Road Block	Mrs Mills
Escape adviser	Ronald Biggs

Ernie is pacing up and down. John enters.

Ernie Major Faversham, sir, Lieutenant D'Arcy is making another attempt to escape.

John Don't get so excited, Captain Hammond. *(Ernie points to each decoration)* VC, DSO, MM, DFC, and bar.

Ernie Thank you, sir, he's trying to escape now.

John I'm sorry to have to say this about a fellow officer but Lieutenant D'Arcy is a fool.

Ernie He wants to escape back to England to fight again.

John That could put another three years on the war. Remember last time he tried to escape? He put black boot polish on his face, took one step outside the hut and the searchlight shone right on him. Stood there and sang 'Mammy'. I wouldn't mind only he sang it so damned badly.

Ernie He's a trier, sir.

John He's trying me to the limits.

Ernie Do you think he'll escape this time, sir?

John I'll let you know if he's escaped in three seconds. *(Looks at watch and counts down)* Three, two, one ...

F/X: rifle shot and Eric's cry of pain.

John No.

Door opens and German commandant, looking very angry, enters.

Officer Major Faversham, as senior officer, I would ask you to assert a little more authority over your men, especially this one. *(Jerks thumb towards door)* He is a fool. Fifteen times he's tried to escape and fifteen times we catch him. *(Shouts through door)* Send in the Swinehund!

Eric enters dressed as nurse.

Eric Evenin' all. Nurse Swinehund reporting. Sorry I'm late, an emergency case. A German bandsman collapsed and I had to take his appendix out with my ukelele.

Officer Did you honestly think you could fool us with such a disguise? *(Starts to pull off Eric's costume)*

Eric *(Pained cry)* That's mine! *(Eric is now in officer's uniform with trouser legs rolled up. Gives wig to Ern)* It didn't work, but thanks a lot.

Officer And the next time you try to escape you'll be shot at dawn.

Eric I'm not worried – and I don't get up till nine o'clock.

Officer Next time you won't get off so lightly. Goodnight, gentlemen, heil Hitler! *(Exits)*

Eric And Luton for the Cup. Wonderful make-up, you'd never dream that was Vera Lynn would you?

Ernie Sit down!

Eric I am sat down.

John D'Arcy, you're a fool.

Eric Will you still call me a fool when I tell you about my brand new plan of escape?

John What is your plan of escape?

Eric Read that. *(Gives letter to John)*

John Very well. *(Reading aloud)* 'To the guard at the gate. The three men what have got this note are ...'

Eric Good, isn't it?

John ' ... very good friends of mine and are to be allowed out through the main gate, signed Adolf Hitler, Boss of Germany.'

Eric *(Very pleased)* What do you think?

John You wrote this?

Eric Who else?

John D'Arcy, this note would never fool the Germans.

Ernie Of course not. Hitler would never use a pencil.

John And secondly he most certainly would not use notepaper headed 'J. Balshaw and Sons, plumbers and decorators, Stockport'.

Eric He is my uncle, sir.

Ernie Just you forget that stupid letter and listen to what our good major has to tell you. Go on, Major.

John D'Arcy. I'd like you to listen very carefully to what I'm going to say. Captain Hammond *(Ern pulls John back)* VC, DSO, MM, DFC, and bar ...

Ernie — Thank you, sir. That stove is the entrance to the tunnel that the good major and myself have been digging.

Eric — Tunnel?

Ernie & John — Ssh!

John — Yes, the captain and I have been digging solidly now for two weeks. And we think it's high time that you did your bit down there.

Eric — That's very kind of you, sir.

Ernie — Get down into that tunnel and start digging.

Moves stove aside.

Eric — Certainly. If the guards start asking questions ...

Ernie — Yes?

Eric — Yes, just tell them that I'm planting King Edwards.

Ernie — Get down there and start digging.

Eric disappears inside the stove ... Door opens and commandant enters.

Officer Gentlemen!

John and Ern look at each other in desperation. John signals for Ern to stand between the stove and the Officer.

John Erm, lovely evening.

Officer I'm not interested in the weather, Major. I have a camp to run. *(Holds up paper)* Roll call.

Ernie Roll call?

John Surely not a roll call.

Officer Just answer your names. Faversham!

John Who?

Officer You, sir, Faversham!

John Oh, here!

Officer Hammond!

Ernie Here! *(Points to medals)*

Officer VC, DFC, MM, DSO, and bar. D'Arcy.

Eric Here!

Officer Where?

Eric Here.

Officer I can't see him.

Eric Down the tunnel!

Officer What was that?

John Ah, erm, yes, erm, he said, 'He's found the flannel'.

Officer Found the flannel.

John He's taking a shower.

Ernie He's in the shower.

Officer I see. Now listen. *(Raps stick on stove ... Eric winces)* I shall be back in five minutes. *(Stubs cigar out on Eric's head)* Five minutes, heil Hitler! *(Exits)*

Ernie Luton for the Cup!

John and Ern move to door. Smoke is coming from stove.

John Get that fool out quick.

Ernie *(Opens stove and helps Eric out)* You nearly did it, that time.

Eric Did what, sir?

John D'Arcy for sheer and complete incompetence you are unsurpassed.

Eric You are very kind, sir.

Ernie What would you do with the man?

John Tell me something, how the he... how did you get your commission?

Eric ENSA, sir.

John ENSA?

Eric I was a lance corporal entertaining the troops and they said to me, 'Don't go on in the second half and we'll make you a lieutenant.'

John What exactly did you do to entertain the troops?

Eric Ventriloquist.

John I beg your pardon?

Eric I was a ventriloquist, sir.

Ernie A ventriloquist?

Eric Yes, that was me then.

Ernie Were you a good ventriloquist?

Eric The gery gest. I was the gest gentriloquist in Great Gritain.

Ernie The gest gentriloquist in Great Gritain?

John Why don't you hag a gottle og geer and mind your own business, you gloody fool.

Eric That's not very nice, sir.

John Shut up! Hammond ...

Eric VC, DSO, MM, DFC, and bar.

Ernie Sir?

John We must get on with the escape. Get down there and start digging.

Ernie Right away, Major, sir. *(Goes inside stove)*

Eric I've a good mind to light it and burn your pips off.

John You'll do nothing of the kind. Let's hope the commandant doesn't come back while he's down that hole.

Commandant enters.

Officer Heil Hitler!

Eric Luton for the Cup!

John Something wrong, Commandant?

Officer Yes, I want another roll call.

Holds up board.

John Again, sir?

Officer Major Faversham.

John Here, sir.

Officer Lieutenant D'Arcy.

Eric Close.

Officer Captain Hammond.

Silence.

Officer Captain Hammond!

Eric He's... he's having a sleep, sir.

Officer Well wake him up. I want a word with him.

John looks desperately at Eric.

Eric Leave everything to me.

Goes to bed and picks up dummy. Brings it between John and himself.

Officer Why didn't he stand up when I came into the room?

Eric He was sleeping like a log, sir.

Officer *(Studying dummy)* Oh. Captain Hammond? How are you today?

Eric *(Vent well)* I'm gery well thank you.

Officer You look a little pale, D'Arcy. Have a glass of water. *(Hands Eric water)*

John *(Whispers to Eric)* Have you ever done it while drinking a glass of water?

Eric There's no answer to that!

Officer Captain Hammond, kindly tell me your name, rank and number.

Eric I can tell you that.

Officer (*To Eric*) You drink! (*To dummy*) Captain Hammond, I want you to tell me your name, rank and number.

Eric almost chokes, whilst trying to speak and drink the water.

John (*Does ventriloquist voice, while Eric drinks and works doll*) Two four two four nought eight two Hammond, Captain.

Commandant looks first at dummy then closely at John.

Eric VC, DSO, MM, DFC and bar.

Officer Very interesting.

John You seem to doubt whether this is Captain Hammond.

Eric There's one sure way to find out.

Officer There is indeed. (*Lifts wig off head of doll*) It is the captain. (*Replaces wig*) Goodnight gentlemen, heil Hitler! (*Exits*)

Eric Luton for the Cup!

Ernie (*From stove*) Get me out of here.

Officer (*Re-enters*) And another thing, gentlemen.

They all get in line – dummy next to Ernie. Commandant looks closely at Ernie and dummy not believing his eyes.

Officer *(Dazed)* I really must take some leave. *(Hand salute)* Luton for the Cup.

John That was a narrow squeak.

Ernie It's hell down there, sir.

Stove is pulled out for Eric to go down.

John It's your turn again, D'Arcy.

Eric Before I go – if I don't come back will you please give this parcel to my wife?

John But you will come back.

Eric In case I don't, please see that my wife gets this parcel.

Ernie But what is it?

Eric A hand grenade.

Eric goes into stove. Doors burst open and British soldier enters.

Soldier The Army's here lads.

John Good heavens, the British Army?

Soldier Yes, sir, the war's over.

Ernie Did we win?

Soldier Yes, sir.

Ernie Oh good, I've won two bob.

John And we're free men again?

Soldier There's a truck waiting outside ready to take all prisoners down to the docks and home.

John Home.

Ernie We're going home.

John & Ernie We're going home.

Cheering, they both exit with soldier.

Eric *(Still in tunnel)* Hey ho, hey ho it's off to work we go. With me shovel and me pick and I've lost me flamin' wick...

Ernie For me John Mills was absolutely superb in that play.

Eric Brilliant. They should give him Colditz after that performance.

Ernie I would go so far as to say he was one of the cleverest actors we've ever had on our shows.

Eric Anyone who makes sure he gets paid before goes on one of our shows has got to be clever.

Ernie John had such superb control.

Eric I liked the way he kept a stiff upper lip when things really looked bad.

Ernie You mean when the Germans discovered him trying to escape?

Eric No, in the BBC Club when it was his turn to get a round in.

Ernie I was just thinking.

Eric What?

Ernie Do you think whoever's reading this now has bought the book or is just flicking through the pages?

Eric Difficult to say. If it's a person of taste flicking through the pages the next bit is sure to make him want to buy the book.

Ernie You mean the piece about 'the connoisseurs'?

Eric Good taste, dignity.

Ernie All of those qualities.

Eric And that's not like you.

Chips with Everything

Whenever we did one of these sketches we always referred to them as 'the connoisseurs' and Allan Cuthbertson was very important in his role of the chairman.

He was a towering figure, well over six feet tall. He also looked and sounded an authoritative man, important for Eric and Ernie to score off as they went about the vitally important business of tasting and approving chips.

We had successfully done an earlier connoisseurs sketch on the merits, or otherwise, of British Rail sausages. There was the revolutionary, first ever in the world 'luminous sausage'. The great advantage was you could see this sausage when the train entered a tunnel, and because of its brilliantly innovative design, it rocked back and forth on the plate and dipped itself in the egg. So you see, the connoisseurs played a very important part in bringing the nation to the quite astonishingly high standard of chips that it enjoys today.

When this sketch was being performed in front of the cameras we had chips brought down from the BBC canteen. They were so tasty that both Eric and Ernie held up the recording for five minutes while they finished eating all the chips. Two more helpings were sent for and the sketch got under way.

We see the chairman on a 'quiz' set: Eric and Ernie are behind a table.

Chairman Good evening. How many times have you marvelled at the knowledge shown by the connoisseurs of good wines? Tonight we'd like you to marvel yet again at the expertise of our two much-travelled guests this evening – both of them connoisseurs of chips. Gentlemen?

Ernie wakes Eric.

Eric Hello.

Ernie Good evening.

Chairman Tonight we have an assortment of chips chosen at random from various fish and chip shops. They are now going to tell us all that they can about the chips by tasting them. When you're ready gentlemen – here is bag number one.

Eric and Ernie now both put on white gloves: the Chairman picks up the first bag and passes it carefully to them. Both nibble a chip and both look very thoughtful as they chew.

Eric A tantalising little chip.

Ernie Very pleasant.

Eric *(Smells his chip)* Good bouquet.

Ernie Excellent vinegar.

Eric *(To chairman)* Malt '67?

Chairman It is indeed malt vinegar 1967. How about the chips?

Eric *(To Ernie)* King Edwards?

Ernie No doubt about it.

Chairman Correct again. Now can you name the shop from which they were bought?

Both are chewing and looking thoughtful.

Eric *(To Ernie)* Big Ada's?

Ernie On the corner of Tarryassan Street?

Eric Yes.

Ernie Wait a minute, these are not Big Ada's.

Eric You could be right. *(Looks at chip)* Ada's are much bigger. She always has them loose on the counter. Ada isn't skinny with it.

Ernie *(To chairman)* Was I right about Tarryassan Street?

Chairman You were right, it is Tarryassan Street.

Eric Tarryassan Street South Slope?

Chairman Correct.

Eric Got it!

Ernie Whose are they?

Eric Lee Wong Fu.

Ernie Of course.

Eric *(To chairman)* Lee Wong Fu, corner of Tarryassan Street.

Chairman Very good indeed. Lee Wong Fu it is.

Eric I thought there was a touch of the orient somewhere.

Chairman Now for bag number two, gentlemen.

Eric and Ernie remove the white gloves and put on a fresh pair of white gloves before taking a chip each from bag. Both chew and look thoughtful.

Chairman Well, gentlemen?

Ernie *(Chewing and thinking as he turns to Eric)* Herbie's in Daglish Avenue?

Eric No. *(Chewing)* It's the vinegar I recognise... on the tip of me tongue... little red-headed fellow owns the shop... used to be in the Navy.

Ernie I know him – walks funny.

Eric Just come out of prison. Ginger Dunn!

Chairman Ginger Dunn is quite right.

Ernie You always get little crispy bits off Ginger.

Eric I should have known. I pass his shop every day on the way to work. Often see him at the back soaking his peas.

Chairman You've done very well up to now. Bag number three, please. This time perhaps you could tell us more about the actual potatoes.

Both change into fresh gloves: from bag three Eric takes a bent chip.

Ernie Good heavens.

Eric Now this is something fantastic.

Chairman You seem enthusiastic.

Eric Do you know what this is?

Chairman Please tell me?

Eric This is a 'Lincolnshire Bender'. Just look at the perfect curve of that chip.

Ernie The work of an artist.

Eric Beautiful that is. Hand cut.

Ernie And unless I'm sadly mistaken that potato has been grown and cut by the Quigley Bros., Spalding.

Eric No doubt about that at all. Just look at the way the eye has been taken out – clean as a whistle.

Ernie And that can mean only one man -Benjiman Quigley.

Eric Benjiman Quigley – MCC.

Chairman MCC?

Eric Master Chipper and Cutter. The Wedgwood of the potato world, he was.

Chairman Was? Do you mean that he...

Eric Very sad. He's now in the great potato patch in the sky.

Ernie 1941 as I remember.

Chairman What happened?

Eric Half of his land in Lincolnshire had been taken over by the War Department.

Ernie And he was very short-sighted.

Eric Ben went out into the field one morning and he tried to peel a hand grenade.

Chairman How tragic.

Eric Yes. They found him the following day up a tree in Huddersfield with his peeler in his hand.

Chairman What a catastrophe.

Ernie You don't see workmanship like this nowadays.

Eric Collector's item this is.

Chairman You've done it again, gentlemen. It is a Lincolnshire Bender. Any particular reason for cutting the chip on the curve like that?

Ernie Stroke of genius on the Quigley Brothers' part.

Eric You see, with it being curved like this, as you're carrying the chips home they rock back and forth in the bag and dip themselves in the vinegar.

Chairman Perhaps you'd like to taste one and give us your comments.

Ernie We'd rather not.

Eric We couldn't eat one because to us as experts it is a work of art and a sheer delight just to look at.

Chairman You've made them sound so delicious I simply must try one. *(Eats a chip)* Very tasty. Now I'd like you both if you would... *(He slumps back)*

Eric and Ern look awkward. Ernie creeps off. Eric shakes the Chairman's hand and exits.

Bed Sketch 2

Ernie is in bed, wearing his pyjamas and writing in a notebook. Eric is on top of the bed, with his dressing gown over pyjamas. He is reading Yoga for Better Health.

Ernie *(Stops writing and looks puzzled)* How do you spell incompetent?

Eric E-R-N-I-E.

Ernie E-R ... *(Realising)* Oh!

Eric Taking shape is it?

Ernie Just got to the part where Inspector Darling of New Scotland Yard has just ...

Eric Who?

Ernie I'm creating a new character, Guy Darling, ace detective. It starts off where he's been followed by two men.

Eric I'm not surprised.

Ernie I've just got to the part where he's arrived at The Grange to arrest the fellow what did it.

Eric To arrest the man what did it?

Ernie My first thriller.

Eric That's long overdue. *(Reads for a few seconds then looks up)* Agatha Crusty.

Ernie Who?

Eric Agatha Crusty. He wrote thrillers.

Ernie Did he?

Eric Oh yes. He wrote that one that's been running in London now for about ninety years... *The Black and White Minstrels.*

Ernie George Mitchell.

Eric I never knew he wrote thrillers!

Ernie looks puzzled, then continues to write. He stops and looks up.

Ernie What's yours like?

Eric Pardon?

Ernie The book.

Eric Yoga.

Ernie That's not for me.

Eric You know a lot about yoga then?

Ernie Only that it's made from milk.

Ernie continues to write... Eric looks puzzled.

Eric *(After a pause)* Indians.

Ernie What about them?

Eric They're good at yoga.

Ernie Oh.

Eric It's a way of life out there. It's their bingo.

Ernie Oh, that sort of yoga. I once read that proper yoga fellows in India can sit cross-legged on the floor for twenty-four hours without moving a muscle.

Eric After four bowls of curry you'd be frightened to move a muscle. Has he arrived at The Grange yet?

Ernie Inspector Darling of New Scotland Yard?

Eric Yes.

Ernie *(Taps notebook)* Just finished that bit. Listen to this... *(Reads from notebook)* Inspector Darling rang the front doorbell. After a pause of some few seconds Lady Angela opened the door with a smile.

Eric That's a good trick.

Ernie *(Still reading)* He entered the study to find Sir Digby, skewered to the floor with a twelve-inch dagger.

Eric Powerful stuff. You could be another – what's his name – you know, they called him 'the bard'.

Ernie The one who wrote all those sonnets and odes?

Eric No, not Cyril Fletcher. There's an exercise here and it says after it in big red letters underlined 'When in this position do not yodel'. The last time I saw a position like that was at the Odeon.

Ernie *(Closes notebook)*
I'm tired.

Eric And no wonder, the way you drive yourself. Words cascade from your pen like pearls from a broken necklace.

Ernie I'm dead beat.

Eric Have you cleaned your tooth?

Ernie I'm going to settle down.

Eric Get married?

Ernie Sleep.

Eric What about Inspector Darling?

Ernie He's just put a tail on the gardener.

Eric That'll keep the flies off his dahlias. *(Laughs)*

Ernie *(Settles down)* Good night, Eric.

Eric *(Looking at yoga book)* By golly some of these positions are impossible – fine if you're a jelly baby. *(Turns book to get a better view of an illustration)* I wouldn't fancy doing that on cold lino. Impossible. *(Closes book and places it on the bedside table)* Goodnight.

Cliff Richard

When it came to the musical spot in the show my contribution was minimal. The song and dance routine was a very important part of the Morecambe & Wise Show. It rounded the overall shape and made it a complete 'entertainment'.

These routines, as I remember from very early shows, started life as easy-paced, very gentle inserts until they became so popular that each dance routine became a major production, and would very often take a full day to record.

'Three American Sailors' is still my favourite dance routine of all time with Eric, Ern and Cliff Richard producing quite dazzling performances to 'The Fleet's In'. This number took much longer than was scheduled because at one point in the routine three mops were thrown on for them to catch while they were dancing. Eric missed his mop and it struck him on the nose causing a slight cut and a visit to the nurse. Ernie was very upset and nurse had to give him a sedative to stop him from laughing. For a great many people 'Singin' in the Rain' is the most popular song and dance routine, with Eric as the waterlogged policeman, Ernie dancing the part that he made famous for Gene Kelly, so he tells me.

When Cliff Richard danced with the boys on the battleship we were all quite surprised at how good he was. I had an ever bigger surprise at his performance prior to the dance routine when he appeared in the flat sketch. I can only repeat what I said at the time: 'I've been looking at a young Cary Grant.' His comedy timing and his delivery really were quite superb. What a pity, and a loss to light comedy, that this part of his repertoire wasn't fully recognised.

Eric is seated on the settee applying the finishing touches with a small paint brush to a model aeroplane. Ernie enters through main door, wearing trendy gear.

Ernie Hello, Eric.

Eric What time will you be back?

Ernie I've just come in.

Eric Been so busy I didn't notice you'd gone.

Continues painting model.

Ernie Eric, I've got some wonderful news.

Eric You've just lost your tap shoes.

Ernie Eric, who would you say is the most popular male singer and entertainer in the country today?

Eric *(Too engrossed to be bothered)* Anita Harris.

Ernie Now think. 'Bachelor Boy', 'Summer Holiday', 'Livin' Doll'.

Eric Give me a clue.

Ernie Cliff ...

Eric Michelmore.

Ernie No. Cliff Richard.

Eric Oh him.

Ernie What do you mean – him? Don't you realise that Cliff wants to come on our show and do a dance routine with us? A dance routine with Cliff Richard.

Ernie gets carried away and starts dance steps: Eric watches.

Eric Sit down you silly old fool.

Ernie I'm not old. *(He sits)*

Eric You do a dance routine with Cliff Richard at your age and you'll make a laughing stock of yourself.

Ernie I can still go a bit I can.

Eric If your name was 'Dobbin' you'd have been in the knacker's yard ten years ago. And look at you – you've only done half a dozen steps and the sweat's standing out on your forehead.

Ernie I'm not sweating.

Eric Then the glue must be running.

Ernie Then you don't want to do a dance number with Cliff?

Eric Where did you meet him?

Ernie He was opening that new discotheque down the road.

Eric Discotheque? You want to keep away from those places. Those Cocoa Dancers are too much for you.

Ernie Cocoa dancers! Way past it you are!

Eric That's right.

Ernie Model aeroplanes – about all you can cope with at your age.

Eric True.

Ernie Well, I'm going to do the dance routine with Cliff. Full of youth and vitality I am.

Eric Not half. You have to swallow a packet of wheat germ to watch *Top of the Pops*.

Ernie Just build your models, grandad.

Ernie starts dancing. Doorbell rings.

Eric If you've got the strength, answer that.

Ernie That'll be Cliff now.

Eric Ask him to hang on for a minute while I stitch the sequins on to your long johns.

Ernie opens door and Cliff enters. Eric carries on painting model.

Ernie Cliff, baby!

Cliff Hello, Ernie. *(Walks over to Eric)* How are you, Eric?

Cliff takes model from Eric: Eric continues painting nothing.

Eric It's taken off! *(Notices Cliff)* Hello – sit down and take the weight off your latest release!

Cliff sits by Eric.

Cliff Did you make this, Eric?

Eric I'm not really very good at it.

Cliff You're kidding. This is beautiful.

Ernie I come on first, Cliff. I'll have to wait a minute or two for the applause to stop...

Cliff Be with you in just a minute, Ernie. Never seen workmanship like this before.

Eric It's a gift. I got the talent from my father. He was an engineer with British Rail – used to weld the crusts on to the meat pies.

Cliff And you've always made models?

Eric Good Lord, yes. *(Points to Ern)* Made him out of a kit. Trouble is I ran out of wood when I got to his legs.

Cliff (*Looks at Ernie*) It's very good – you can't see the join.

Eric You're not going to do many of them, are you? I wouldn't like there to be any friction between us.

Ernie This is what I had in mind, Cliff.

He puts a record on and we hear 'Livin' Doll'.

Eric Take that thing off. You know I can't stand him.

Ernie Cliff's sitting right next to you and you insult one of his records. I'm fed up with you.

Cliff What's the matter with Eric?

Ernie He's in a bad mood tonight. Ask him why he won't do the dance routine.

Cliff Eric, why won't you do the dance routine?

Eric Well, all I want to do at night is put on my slippers, light my pipe, build my models ...

Ernie And watch *Match of the Day*.

Eric What? Who said that? I don't want to watch that.

Ernie I knew it. *Match of the Day* – it's on tonight. That's why he won't do the dance routine, Cliff.

Eric That's got nothing to do with you. I want to finish off this model.

Ernie You're like a six-year-old child.

Eric *(Picks up model plane and pretends it's in flight and that he is the pilot)* Come in B for Charlie! B for Charlie! 'Bandits' at six o'clock and *The Archers* at a quarter to seven.

Ernie Look, Cliff, to do this routine we need three people – will you see if you can get him to do the dance.

Cliff Eric, will you do the routine as a special favour – for me.

Eric Well, seeing as how you put it like that Cliff, – no.

Ernie Knew he'd say that.

Eric I have got these models to finish.

Cliff Eric, if you're only one-tenth as good at dancing as you are at making models, yours could be one of the greatest talents ever seen on the TV screen.

Eric Pardon?

Ernie *(Quietly to Cliff)* You've got him now.

Cliff If you're only one-tenth as good at dancing as you are at making models, yours could be one of the greatest talents ever seen on the TV screen.

Eric Well ...

Cliff Just to satisfy me would you do a couple of steps now?

Eric I don't mind giving you a little treat.

Does a couple of steps and returns to settee.

Cliff You have no right to keep a talent like that to yourself. That wasn't dancing.

Eric What do you mean?

Cliff That was 'leg poetry'.

Ernie Oh, yes.

Cliff You make Pan's People look like a gang of navvies.

Eric There's no answer to that!

Cliff Your dancing ability has been well fostered – you've obviously been nurtured.

Eric *(Leans in to Ernie)* Isn't that what they do to tom-cats?

Cliff The world has a right to enjoy your talent.

Eric *(Gets up)* What are we waiting for, Ern? Cliff and I are waiting to do the routine.

Ernie Great. Got it all worked out, Cliff. You do the song and Eric and I will do all the movements behind you.

Cliff moves the chair, table, and settee.

Cliff Any particular song?

Ernie That latest hit you've got – 'Livin' Doll'.

Cliff Latest hit?

Ernie You must have heard it – he's never off the radio.

Eric You know the one.

Eric goes to piano and plays 'Livin' Doll'. Cliff is horrified at the noise. Eric continues: Cliff walks away.

Ernie You recognise it?

Cliff Oh, yes – it's in there somewhere.

Eric Let's rehearse it.

Both take up positions behind Cliff

Ernie Any time you like, Cliff.

Cliff Yes. Ready?

Both Ready.

Cliff opens his mouth to sing the song and gets only first couple of words out.

Ernie Just a moment!

Eric He's gone wrong.

Ernie No, he hasn't got a microphone.

Eric gets a banana, with string tied round it for a cable: Eric 'tests' the banana for sound, and gives it to Cliff. Cliff sings 'Livin' Doll' while Eric and Ernie start dancing. Cliff stops singing and watches the boys, looking rather worried.

Cliff Boys, I don't know how to say this.

Eric Don't say anything.

Ernie We know it's good.

Cliff Yes, it's ... but don't you think ... what you're doing is a little old-fashioned.

Long horrified pause.

Cliff What I mean is ... I'm singing a

sort of new type of song and your routine is very old.

Another long pause.

Cliff I mean ... in any case, I saw you do the same thing with Tom Jones.

Both Who?

Cliff Tom Jones.

Ernie Oh, that six-footer, curly hair, well set up.

Eric Thought that was Nina.

Cliff Can we do one of Ernie's plays?

Ernie No.

Moves right with disgust.

Eric You've offended him now.

Cliff I was thinking of something a bit more 'with it' – like this.

Cliff dances.

Eric We don't want to get laughs!

Ernie Three American sailors on board a battleship doing a dance routine with mops.

Eric Never been done before.

Cliff Never been done before! But didn't I see Gene Kelly do that in a film?

Ernie Never.

Eric Gene Kelly. She'd never dress up as an American sailor.

Ernie Not now that she's Princess Grace of Meccano.

Cliff I didn't realise.

Eric Be guided by us.

Cliff Well all right then, we'll do it your way. But are you sure it's going to work?

Eric takes the banana from him and eats it.

Eric If you're really worried we'll get that singing group at the back of you – Olivier, Newton and John. Three nice fellows. Who's playing on *Match of the Day* tonight?

Ernie Luton!

Eric Swine!

Ernie Lights ... Music ... Action.

Ernie	Made a pleasant change to work with a really swingin' young pop idol.
Eric	Cliff Richard said those very words to me as well.
Ernie	Cliff suprised me in that play.
Eric	I told him to be careful with the umbrella.
Ernie	I meant he can really act. Just a little more style, a little more sophistication and he could well be another me.
Eric	Never.
Ernie	No. I suppose you're right.
Eric	I'll tell you something now and I mean this.
Ernie	Go on.
Eric	I'm not given to compliments but you look younger than Cliff Richard.
Ernie	Honestly?
Eric	I mean that.
Ernie	Gosh!
Eric	And I reckon Cliff's about sixty-eight now.

Legs Legs

DR SHANKS
LEG
REJUVENATING
MACHINE

DR SHANKS
LEG
REJUVENATING
MACHINE

DR SHANKS
LEG
REJUVENATING
MACHINE

Flora Robson

When the very elegant, very talented Dame Flora Robson swept through the curtains to join Eric and Ernie for the pre-sketch dialogue, it must have been one of the most nervous moments I have experienced as a writer. Dame Flora was wearing the actual costume that she wore as Elizabeth the First in the film *Fire over England.*

I saw the film when I was seven years old. Her co-star was Laurence Olivier. As she entered wearing that stunning gown she looked so very gracious, so dignified. And she was every inch the monarch as she stood looking straight ahead with great authority and, would you believe, carrying a football?

Now can you understand why I felt so nervous? Not only had I written this into the script for this great lady, this international star, I had also written an opening line for her that was to prove a watershed for every guest star who would appear in future Morecambe & Wise Shows.

Looking back now I wouldn't call them insulting lines. They were observations that pricked the star bubble, showed the public that even mega-stars are human.

It was the reaction to Dame Flora's opening line that was so very important to future scripts, and this was the all-important line.

Flora   Sorry I'm late, only I went into the wrong studio and a young man kept asking me if I'll be fit for Saturday.

Eric   And will you?

The audience reaction to this line was more than we had hoped for. It was as if she had said to them, 'Look, I'm really quite ordinary. Like you I'm here for a laugh.'

There were quite a number of laughs during that sketch.

Dame Flora got quite a big laugh on the first day of rehearsal when she asked me if I was related to Lady Brabourne.

Scene: The drawing room of a tastefully furnished country house. Eric and Ernie enter through a sliding door. Ernie takes a couple of cautious steps into room, looks around and calls to Eric.

Ernie You can come in, Eric. The house is empty.

Eric enters and looks round.

Eric Beautiful.

Ernie It's perfect for what we want. Don't forget we've only got the loan of this house for a very short time.

Eric You think this place is going to impress Dame Flora Robson?

Ernie Of course it will, that's the whole idea. When she sees this big, posh house, she'll think that it belongs to me. She'll think that I must be a successful writer and then she'll agree to appear in my play.

Eric Well, I must say, it is a lovely house.

Ernie What period do you think it is?

Eric Well I would say it's either early Tudor or late Wimpey. It really is beautiful.

Ernie I know it is, but the fellow who let me have the key said we must be out as quickly as possible.

Eric *(Picking up vase from mantelpiece)* Hey, Ern, this is a lovely antique.

Ernie Be careful with that!

Eric Oh I will, I'm very interested in antiques, never miss *Going for a Song* with Anna Neagle.

Ernie Arthur Negus.

Eric Is she? Does he know?

Ernie Now, you're going to help me?

Eric Yes. You want me to play the part of your butler.

Ernie Yes. Do a butler's walk.

Eric does so, comes across to Ernie.

Eric How do I look?

Ernie Very nice. *(Eric's shirt front rolls up)* Is that the best you could get?

Eric Yes. I got it from my fishmonger in Harpenden and he wants it back to put in the window. He's out of plaice.

Wanders over to French windows.

Ernie He'll have it back by then, don't worry.

Eric *(Looking out of window)* It's a nice view. Hey, that's a bit naughty. *(Looking out)* I thought you only saw that kind of thing on the Continent.

Ernie I'm not with you.

Eric Come over here and I'll show you. *(Ernie joins him at window)* They've got a pond and standing on the edge of the pond, they've got a statue of a nude figure and he's ... it's the gardener. That's not nice, sir. That's a nasty habit you've got there.

Ernie Never mind him. Now when Dame Flora arrives, announce her, take her coat and above all show respect because she's a gracious lady. Now we've got to get her to appear in my play then we hop it quick before the real owner gets back.

Sound of two blasts on motor horn.

Eric Pardon?

Same two blasts on horn.

Eric You said that without moving your lips.

Ernie *(Looking through window)* It's Dame Flora just getting out of a car.

Eric *(Walking towards door)* I'll go and let her in. *(Exits through sliding doors)*

Ernie Don't forget to announce her and be respectful.

Eric Just a moment, love, I'm coming. Welcome to Mr Wise's residence. Would you follow me, Mrs Dame.

Eric returns and stands by doors.

Eric My lords, ladies and gentlemen, pray silence for the right honourable Dame Flora Robson, she's only here for the ...

Ernie Quiet!

Dame Flora enters. She holds a parasol on her shoulder. Eric closes sliding door behind her as she walks forward – the parasol is cut in half and she is left holding just a stick.

Ernie Dame Flora, I'm delighted to meet you.

Dame Flora Are you Mr Wise?

Ernie Most of the time. *(Takes her hand)*

Eric Could I have your coat please?

Ernie You got my message then, Dame Flora.

Dame Flora Yes I did. When I arrived here at the airport, inviting me to have drinks with you in this house.

Eric Could I have your coat please, sweetheart?

Ernie It is rather a beautiful house, isn't it?

Dame Flora I'm rather surprised to see you in such beautiful surroundings.

Ernie Well you see, Dame Flora, when one is a successful writer, like what I am, one can afford a residence like this.

Eric Look, are you going to give me that coat or not?

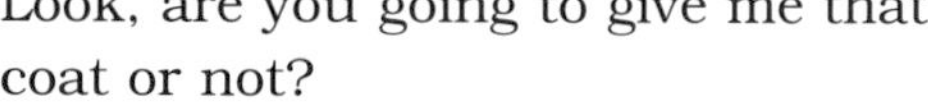

Ernie You like my little place then Dame Flora?

Dame Flora I do. I like it very much indeed, Mr Wise. When I received your note I ...

(Stops because Eric is pulling at the sleeve of her coat, trying to remove it)

Ernie Eric, please!

Dame Flora Oh, I'm so sorry. I didn't realise you were waiting to take my coat.

Eric helps her to remove her coat.

Eric The heating is full on you know.

Ernie This is Eric, my butler. The old family retriever.

Dame Flora *(Mystified)* Family retriever?

Eric It's the ears that do it. If you whistle for me five miles away, I'll come running.

Ernie That's right. *(Turns back on Eric as he indicates that Dame Flora be seated on the settee)* Dame Flora, please be sat down.

Eric puts her coat over Ernie's shoulders.

Dame Flora *(Sits)* Thank you.

Ernie As you may know Dame Flora, I have written an absolutely brilliant play.

Ernie sits on settee next to Dame Flora.

Ernie I've written it specially for you and I've called it ...

Dame Flora You've got my coat on, Mr Wise.

Ernie No, that's not the title. *(Realises)* Oh, I'm most terribly, awfully sorry. *(Ernie rises, Eric helps him off with coat. Eric folds coat and puts it on settee, Ernie sits on it)*. You have a coat like this haven't you, Dame Flora? So sorry Dame Flora, everything's slightly adjacent today.

Dame Flora *(Mystified)* Slightly adjacent?

Ernie I'm glad you've noticed.

Dame Flora Tell me about your play, Mr Wise.

Ernie It's historical and also it takes place in the past.

Eric *(From French window)* I've told you once to stop that. Dame Flora's here – have a bit of respect.

Dame Flora What's going on out there?

Eric *(Coming across to Dame Flora)* Come and have a look for yourself.

Ernie *(Quickly cuts in and takes Eric to window)* Will you stop that?

Eric Well tell me what you want me to do.

Ernie Well you're a butler, go and buttle. Wait till I go back to Dame Flora, then come over and ask us if we'd like a drink.

Eric No problem, Ern.

Ernie Good. *(Starts to walk back to Dame Flora)*

Eric *(Shouting)* Does anyone fancy a jar?

Ernie *(To Eric)* Not yet! *(Sits next to Dame Flora)* Sorry about that.

Dame Flora I wonder, Mr Wise, could you give me a little more detail about your play. I don't wish to hurry you but I do have a car waiting outside.

Eric Cigar?

Ernie *(To Dame Flora)* This is one of my perks. Twelve a day.

Eric cuts the cigar and Ernie is left with the short piece of the cigar.

Ernie We're so pleased that you are considering appearing in my play, and we're even more delighted that you've agreed to do it for nothing.

Dame Flora *(Taken aback)* I'm doing it for nothing?

Ernie That's very kind of you.

Eric That was a clever one, Ern. Could I have the keys to the wine closet, please?

Ernie They're in my pocket. Excuse me, Dame, Dame Flora.

Gives Eric the end of a key chain. Through the next speech Eric moves over to drinks cabinet and we see a very long piece of string being pulled out of Ern's pocket.

Ernie I've always been an ardent admirer of your work, the chance to work with you has always been my greatest ambition. *(Ernie is pulled completely off settee)* I'm terribly sorry, I slipped off the settee.

Dame Flora Have you hurt yourself?

Ernie No. Only when I laugh.

Dame Flora How long have you lived in this house, Mr Wise?

Ernie Ever since I became a highly successful writer. All my life.

Dame Flora I see.

Eric *(Giving a bottle and glasses to Dame Flora)* Would you mind holding these?

Eric is setting table and drinks during next speech.

Ernie About my play, Dame Flora. It deals with Her Most Gracious Majesty Queen Elizabeth I.

Dame Flora That sounds very interesting. I've always thought that the reign of Queen Elizabeth I covered one of the most colourful periods in our history.

Eric Would you care for a drink, sir.

Ernie Ladies first.

Eric I know. Would you care for a drink, sir?

Ernie Thank you.

Eric Say when, sir. *(Starts pouring)*

Ernie *(Ignoring Eric)* I quite agree with you that this is a most interesting part of our history and in the way I've written this play I have tried to bring out the characters of not only Queen Elizabeth but the people surrounding her at court.

Eric *(Interrupting)* There's a man coming to give you some money.

Ernie When?

Eric *(Stops pouring)* Never fails. *(Turns to Dame Flora)* Would you like a quick snort my lord?

Ernie *(Aside)* Oh God.

Dame Flora I beg your pardon?

Eric Would you care for a drop of falling-down water?

Dame Flora Yes, a little please. *(Eric pours)* Thank you, that's plenty.

Eric It's all you're going to get. I can recommend it – it's the eighty-three.

Dame Flora Eighty-three?

Eric Eighty-three bottles for fifteen and nine.

Ernie Here's to a happy association. *(They clink glasses and drink)*

Eric Would you like a little more?

Ernie Just a little touch.

Eric Later. But are you going to have some more drink?

Ernie Yes please. *(Eric pours)*

Eric *(To Dame Flora)* How about you your reverence?

Dame Flora *(Placing hand over top of glass)* No, I don't think so.

Eric pours drink and it goes over Dame Flora's hand.

Eric I do beg your pardon, my lord. *(Shakes Dame Flora's hand over bottle)*

Ernie You stupid idiot.

Eric I shouldn't stand for that. Did it go over your dress?

Dame Flora No, it didn't touch my dress. It went over my hand and melted the strap of my wristwatch.

Eric *(To Ern)* We've got a right one here. I told you it was good. One glass of that stuff and you'll break the sound barrier.

Dame Flora Mr Wise, I hope you don't think it's discourteous of me but I do have a car waiting outside.

Ernie Then I'll come straight to the point, Dame Flora. I want you to star as Queen Elizabeth I in my play of the same name called Good Queen Bess.

Dame Flora It's most kind of you, Mr Wise, but I don't know...

She rises but is stopped by Eric who climbs over settee and sits between Ernie and Dame Flora.

Eric If I might put in a word here, my lord. Mr Wise here of whom it has been said ...

Dame Flora It has?

Eric Oh yes, many times. Haven't you heard? Some time ago Mr Wise wrote an historical play which also took place in the past, are you listening to me?

Dame Flora Yes.

Eric Well look at me while you're listening. Mr Wise wrote an historical play about King Arthur starring the one and only ... *(To Ernie)* What was his name?

Ernie Peter Cushing.

Eric Peter Cushing.

Dame Flora A very fine actor.

Ernie Yes, Peter Cushing, he was in it.

Eric Never been more in it than he was that night. Peter Cushing appeared in one of his plays and as a result he now has his own firewood round.

Ernie That's perfectly true, Dame Flora.

Eric Now answer me truthfully, how many famous actors do you know of that have their own firewood round?

Dame Flora I must admit not very many.

Eric There you are then.

Ernie *(Proudly)* And all through being in one of my plays.

Eric You'll never believe this but Peter Cushing is now clearing fourteen to fifteen quid a week on that firewood round.

Dame Flora That's not peanuts.

Ernie No expense, no overheads.

Eric Just a little cart and a chopper and on the side of the cart he's got written 'The Sherlock Homes Firewood Company'.

Ernie *(Proudly)* I did that for him.

Dame Flora I'm sure you did.

Eric: If you play your cards right he could do the same for you.

Dame Flora: I honestly don't think I could do it, Mr Wise.

Ernie: *(Gets up looking very disappointed)* Oh.

Eric: *(Getting up)* Just look at his face, you've shattered him now.

Dame Flora: I'm sorry I ...

Eric: You've set his career back 20 years with that refusal. In my opinion the play he's written for you is the finest work since Peter Osgood wrote *Look Back in Anger*.

Ernie: John Osborne.

Eric: He plays for Chelsea. He knows nothing, this lad.

Ernie: You'll never know how disappointed I feel now.

Dame Flora: I'm sorry.

Ernie: Had you agreed to appear in one of my plays I'd have been able to say that I'd reached my pinnacle.

Eric: And he doesn't do that very much these days. However – Ernie, it doesn't matter.

Dame Flora: It does matter, Mr Wise, it matters a lot to me and I won't have you upset like this – all right, I'll be delighted to appear in your play.

Ernie (*Delighted*) You will!

Dame Flora I'll be honoured to speak your words Mr Wise. (*Rises*) Now I must go. The car is outside.

Ernie (*Takes Dame Flora's hand*) Looking forward to having you in my play, Dame Flora. We'll be in touch.

Dame Flora I look forward to that. Goodbye. (*Exits*)

Eric (*Pulls her back*) It's raining like mad outside, you'll need this. (*Hands her stick of parasol. Dame Flora reacts then exits*)

Eric Happy now, Ern?

Ernie Gosh, I'll say! I'll be happier still when we get out of this house. Let's go now before the real owner gets back.

Chauffeur enters.

Chauffeur Where do you want the luggage?

Dame Flora enters.

Dame Flora Just there. (*Chauffeur exits*) Oh it's good to be home again.

Ernie (*Quietly to Eric*) It's Dame Flora's house.

They both edge towards door.

Dame Flora Boys, please don't go, stay and have some of my drink. (*Takes bottle from Eric*) It's the eighty-three.

Both Eighty-three?

Dame Flora Eighty-three bottles for fifteen and nine.

Eric and Ernie give sickly smiles and slowly exit.

Ernie After that performance by Dame Flora I've got to admit you were right.

Eric Course I was. I told you when you first started to write that play about Queen Elizabeth that Dame Flora was a better bet than Larry Grayson.

Ernie I suppose he does go over the top.

Eric Just a bit. When you write your life story don't forget to say that you had one of the all time greats in one of your plays.

Ernie I will.

Eric And make sure you spell my name right.

Ernie Dame Flora Robson is a perfectionist – the magnificent costume she wore in that play.

Eric Proper regal robes of the period they were.

Ernie Anyone could see that.

Eric Six hours she was in the launderette with that lot.

Ernie Dame Flora looked absolutely magnificent, beautiful frock that was.

Eric More sequins on that frock than you'll see in sixteen programmes of *Come Dancing*.

Ernie We've been very lucky, Eric. The great stars we've had working with us. Dame Flora and next the great Glenda Jackson as Cleopatra.

Eric A fine lady actor.

Ernie You see if I'm not right, one of these days they'll make Glenda a Dame.

Eric No, she won't do pantomime now. She's internationally famous now, she's got half as many awards as you.

Ernie Didn't know she was that good.

Eric She's got two Oscars.

Ernie Didn't even know she was married. I do know she did a very good job as Cleopatra in my play of the same name.

Eric What was the play called?

Ernie I think it was *Cleopatra*.

Eric Oh.

Ernie She gave my work a certain tone, a certain dignity.

Eric So that's what ruined it.

Glenda Jackson

My daughters, Jane and Clare, once bought me a most acceptable birthday present, a very small and compact Dictaphone. Quite honestly, I was tickled many shades of pink with this gift because with this gadget, something I had seen so many times being used in Hollywood films, I could now play at being the Private Eye. You know the sort of thing: switch the machine on, push your trilby to the back of your head, shake a cigarette out of the packet, light up, all done with one hand before speaking into the machine with an American accent. 'My name is Marlowe, Phillip Marlowe private eye, my other eye's just slipped out for a minute.' However, it wasn't bought for me to play games with. It was to stop me from disturbing my wife in the middle of the night when I woke up and fumbled with the light switch so that I could jot down the key words of a gag that had just made itself known to me. Now that I had the Dictaphone at the side of the bed all I had to do was speak quietly into the machine and Deidre could sleep serenely on. Unfortunately it didn't quite work that way.

It was two-thirty in the morning when she sat up in bed, and I thought that she sounded a touch agitated when she said, 'Centurion.'

Pardon'

Centurion

Where?

You just said centurion

Oh it's for a joke

I don't think it's funny.

A short grunt, a tug of the duvet, then she turned her back on me without hearing my newborn gag.

It eventually saw the light of the television screen in the Cleoptra sketch with Glenda Jackson, quite a remarkable lady. It was winning the second Academy Award that got her on the show, one wouldn't have been enough.

Pleasantly, I recall talking to her in the BBC studio just minutes before she was due to rehearse the Cleopatra. We were swapping stories about our mutual Merseyside, and as we spoke I was looking at Glenda and thinking, 'What's so special about you? You don't look glamorous. You don't look a bit like a film star. This is like talking to an ordinary housewife'. Then she was called to take up her position in front of camera: 'action,' then it happened, as though a button marked 'magic' had been pressed. The transformation was instantaneously magical and I was now looking at a star.

Glenda has more than once said of her appearance on the show that it was one of the happiest times in her career. It's difficult to doubt that comment as I remember how mightily she fought to stop from laughing during the Cleopatra sketch when Eric was doing the ventriloquist routine with the bust of Caesar.

Thank you Glenda Jackson, MP. Marvellous Performer.

Antony & CLEOPATRA

Queen Cleopatra – Glenda Jackson
Mark Antony – Ernie Wise
Desdemona – Ann Hamilton
Octavian Caesar – Eric Morecambe
Little Caesar – Edward G. Robinson
Galley Slave – Sir Francis Chichester
King of Mecca – Eric Morley

1st Camel – Englebert Humperdinck
2nd & 3rd Camels – Peggy Mount and Yoko Ono Himself
Miss Jackson's wardrobe by Steptoe & Son
Mr Wise's wigs by the Acme Carpet Company
Special effects by The Highland Whisky Distillers Ltd
Dialogue coach Charlie Chester

Scene: A richly furnished apartment in Cleopatra's palace. Main item of furniture is a divan piled high with cushions. Across centre background are richly coloured curtains which, when drawn back, would show a view of the desert Sphinx. The curtains are closed at the back of the set.

Ann My Queen Cleopatra will be receiving Mark Antony soon. *(Begins to tidy cushions on divan)* My queen is beautiful but ruthless. Mark Antony loves her most dearly, like all men he just melts before the fire of her beauty! *(Listens)* My queen is here now!

Glenda enters as Cleopatra and we hear signature music of Dr Finlay's Casebook. Glenda looks puzzled. She raises her hand.

Glenda There you are, Desdemona.

Ann My queen.

Glenda Has my lover arrived yet?

Ann Which one?

Glenda What day is it?

Ann Friday.

Glenda *(Looks at diary)* Mark Antony. Two 'til ten.

Ann He loves you terribly.

Glenda I keep telling him that. All men are fools, Desdemona. They place themselves at my feet and I use them as stepping stones.

Trumpet – Roman Fanfare

Ann It's Mark Antony, my queen.

Glenda Another stepping stone arriving. Go and help him up the steps, he's only got little legs.

Ann He is here now. Mark Antony!

Ernie enters to signature tune of Z Cars; *looking puzzled. When he raises his hand the music stops. He crosses to Glenda on knees.*

Ernie My queen. *(Kisses Glenda's hand)* I search in vain for words adequate enough to describe your beauty.

Glenda Try.

Ernie How's this for starters? I have only loved like this once before. When I die you will find engraved upon my heart the words 'Cleopatra' and 'Barclays Bank'.

Glenda I can honestly say that I've never heard such flattering words. Would you leave us, Desdemona?

Ann My queen. *(Bows and exits)*

Ernie Alone at last! Get the grapes out and let's get at it!

He Jumps at Glenda but she moves. Ernie lands on divan.

Glenda Are you quite sure that we are alone?

Ernie Of course we're alone.

Glenda I think not. For some time now I have had the feeling that we are being watched.

Ernie Impossible!

Glenda You think so?

Crosses to curtains centre background and pulls them back. We see Eric looking through the hole in the Sphinx where the face of the Sphinx should be.

Ernie Oh he's so far away. He can't see us from there.

Eric picks up a telescope. Glenda closes the curtains.

Ernie Who was that?

Glenda I believe him to be a Roman guard, a soldier sent to my palace by Julius Caesar with strict orders to watch me and the company I keep.

Ernie If Julius Caesar gets to know that you and I have been...

Glenda It would mean death for us both.

Ernie And that's not nice, is it?

Glenda Don't worry. I can deal with him.

Ann enters.

Ann My queen! The Roman guard is here!

Eric enters to signature music of Match of the Day. *He is dressed as a gladiator and wearing Wellington boots and a busby. Fade music. Ann exits.*

Eric Evenin' all! Sorry I'm late only I've been irrigating the desert – takes a bit of doing on your own.

Glenda Is Caesar with you?

Eric No he couldn't come. He's got the hieroglyphics.

Glenda You must be hungry after such a long journey – can I get you some food?

Eric Thank you all the same but I've just had a couple of sheep's eyes – they'll see me through the day.

Glenda *(Seductively)* But you must be hungry for something.

Eric That's true.

Ernie And what is your business here?

Eric I have been sent from Julius and Caesar.

Glenda Julius and Caesar?

Eric I'm afraid so – a slight accident whilst polishing his sword.

Glenda Am I right in assuming that you have been sent here with the sole object of spying on me?

Eric Is there anything to spy on?

Glenda Meaning?

Eric You and the little chap here, have you been ... touch of the hello folks.

Ernie Good heavens no, sir! How could you think such a thing! Nothing of that

nature going on here I do assure you most sincerely.

Glenda All men are fools, and what makes them so is having beauty like what I have got.

Ernie You have a plan?

Glenda Let me have five minutes alone with him. If I can incriminate him we need have no fear of what he can do.

Ernie He is a dedicated Roman soldier and you will never implicate him.

Glenda Leave me alone with him.

Ernie *(To Eric)* Would you like me to attend to your camel?

Eric It's outside – can't miss it – looks like a horse with an air lock. *(Gives Ernie the hat)* Put this on his hump in case it freezes during the night.

Ernie Right away! *(Exits)*

Eric A remarkable beast.

Glenda The camel?

Eric No, Ern.

Oboe plays oriental music as Glenda moves seductively to the bed.

Eric Is your back still bad?

Glenda I like you.

Eric Hello.

Glenda You're a warm-blooded type and you're driving me mad with desire. I am aflame with passion and I can feel myself getting hotter every second.

Eric Leave everything to me, cheeky.

He takes a frond to use as a fan. All leaves drop off as he shakes it.

Glenda Is this your first visit to Egypt?

Eric Never been here before in my life.

Glenda When was that?

Eric I think we've turned over two pages. About two years ago.

Both look puzzled.

Glenda What do you think of the pyramids?

Eric Excellent – their last record was a belter.

Glenda *(Sits)* I'm sure that you'll find it more comfortable on these cushions – next to me.

Eric *(Reads from scroll)* Lady, I must warn you that I am a soldier of Rome and that I have sworn a vow to my Emperor. If you are toying with the idea of trying to seduce me I must tell you that I will have no alternative other than to leave this room first thing tomorrow morning – move up.

He sits next to Glenda. Glenda reaches for the grapes. Eric gets up with grapes and goes behind the bed. Puts grapes on floor. Treads them quickly. Bends down and picks up a glass of wine.

Eric *(Gives Glenda the glass)* There you are.

Glenda Sit down.

Eric I am sat down.

Glenda Would you like to rest your head on my lap?

Eric If you can get it off, of course. *(Rests head on Glenda's lap)*

Glenda Don't you find the desert romantic?

Eric It's all right now but what's it like when the tide comes in?

Glenda I like you. Kiss me.

Eric Well all right then.

Glenda Comfortable?

Eric Just a minute. *(Reaches under cushions and brings out Glenda's Oscar)* Yours I believe?

Ernie enters with a pedestal. He kneels behind divan and rests his head on pedestal.

Glenda Sorry. *(Takes Oscar and places it to one side)* Now then ... *(Begins to stroke Eric's hair. Ernie is watching, between them)* Do you like me stroking your hair?

Eric Don't stroke it too hard – I've only got four left and three of them are Ernie's.

Ernie *(To Glenda, through the side of his mouth)* Put the sleeping powder in his goblet.

Glenda *(Side of mouth)* I beg your pardon?

Ernie The sleeping powder in his goblet – then we can sling him in the Nile.

Glenda *(To Eric)* Oh, another drink?

She takes goblet from table and empties powder from ring. Eric listens. Glenda turns and gives the goblet to Eric. She turns back to the table to get her own drink. Eric throws contents over his shoulder into Ernie's face. Ernie does business of going to sleep.

Glenda How long is it since you last saw a woman?

Eric I've forgotten, sir! *(He tries to free himself from Glenda)*

Glenda *(Holding Eric down)* It's no use trying to fight me. I can feel your heart pounding like a whippet inside a bowler hat.

Eric *(Rises quickly)* Oh, but you are having an affair with Mark Antony.

Glenda *(Rises in anger)* Me and Mark Antony? Don't mention that man's name to me. I can't stand the sight of him!

Ernie *(Out from behind pedestal in anger)* I heard that! I heard what you said about me and I'm not having that! It's time for me to act.

Glenda That'll be the day.

Eric You loved this lady?

Ernie I loved her once.

Eric Once? I thought you were a centurion. You're all talk you are.

Glenda Mark Antony, you have been and always will be a fool!

Ernie You've been using me as a big prawn!

Eric You can't fight nature.

Glenda *(Arms around Eric's neck)* I love you and I want you to take me with you to Rome.

Ernie She lies! And what makes her so is having beauty like what she has got.

Ann rushes on.

Ann My queen.

Glenda What is it, Desdemona?

Eric Desdemona? She looks more like Des O'Connor.

Ann My queen, terrible news from abroad.

Eric I knew it, they want the Oscar back.

Glenda Speak, Desdemona.

Ann If you return to Rome with that man you will die.

Glenda Is this true?

Eric As surely as the desert sun rises above the Co-op in Cairo.

Glenda Who are you?

Eric I am Octavian Caesar. Nephew of Julius and Caesar. Ruler of all the world including parts of Birkenhead.

Ernie Julius Caesar's nephew? I can't believe it.

Ann Now do you see why he wants to take you back to Rome?

Glenda As his prisoner – to face Julius and Caesar and certain death.

Eric *(To Ernie)* You have been having an affair with the queen!

Glenda It was nothing!

Eric I can believe that!

Glenda Then you intend seeing this through to the bitter end?

Eric Might as well – we've learned all the words.

Glenda I have one final request.

Eric Well hurry up because we're running late.

Ernie A final request?

Glenda If I am to die I'd like to do it by my own hand.

Ann *(Sobbing)* No!

Eric A fine actor, that boy. Another contract.

Glenda Fetch me the asp.

Ann gets a basket from the side. She puts it down and exits sobbing.

Glenda This is the end for me.

Eric She's got an asp in that basket.

Glenda Would you hold the basket while I remove the lid? This deadly serpent will put an end to my misery by biting me on the breast.

Eric takes the basket, and both he and Ernie react.

Eric Could I have a word with you please? *(They whisper)*

Glenda *(Parts her dress at the top and closes her eyes for the 'bite')* End it for me now!

Eric's hand comes snake-like out of the top of the basket.

Ernie What are you doing?

Eric Just warming the snake up.

Ernie You're disgusting you are!

Eric Of course I am!

Glenda *(Eyes still closed)* Put me out of my misery.

Eric Any second now. Ready?

Glenda Ready!

Glenda starts to die.

Eric No, too early! Now!

Eric's snake-like hand bites Glenda and she dies a slow death on the cushions.

Eric Is she dead?

Ernie Yes.

Eric Good, now's me chance. *(Takes the Oscar from behind cushions)* I'm going to pinch her Oscar.

Eric Happy with that play, Ern?

Ernie Perfectly. It was beautifully written.

Eric And Glenda?

Ernie Quite happy. She came up to my expectations.

Eric You were standing on a box.

Ernie What an actress.

Eric Glenda has that ... I'm not sure what you call it but it's caused through sleeping with a tight hairnet on.

Ernie On an equally serious note I did change my style of writing for the next play.

Eric If I remember rightly you didn't so much change your style of writing as your position because of the rash.

Ernie That had nothing to do with it. I used a completely new technique in my play which took a look at what our future might be in a work of mine called *Ten Years Hence.*

Eric I remember that play. You were nominated for that one – I would have done it myself if I could have found a chisel.

Ten Years Hence

What would happen to Morecambe and Wise if they ever split up? A journalist once asked me that question during an interview for a newspaper. It was an unthinkable question to ask at a time when they were so enormously popular. That was probably why he asked it.

By asking that question he led me to think what the Eric and Ernie I had created would do if they decided to go their separate ways, called a halt to the partnership and quit show business. When I was mapping the sketch out I started off from an illogical angle, with Eric as the one who had made a success of life without his partner and Ernie as the unfortunate one who had fallen on hard times and was up to his neck in debt. After only half a dozen lines it was painfully obvious that this device would never work, why I thought it would is still a mystery.

This 'mini-play' – that's what a lot of the sketches we did were – was almost a breakthrough for Eric and Ernie because they really did have to act; no ad-libs or the whole piece would fall apart.

It worked very well for both of them with, as always, an immaculate performance by Ann Hamilton as Eric's shrewd, no-nonsense wife.

Here's quite an amazing fact: in the fourteen years that I had the privilege of writing for Morecambe & Wise, never once did they forget a line in front of camera, at least not in my presence. Now that really is quite an achievement when you consider all the opening spots, all the quickies and all the major sketches that they had to remember.

That really is total and absolute professionalism.

The year is 1981. Morecambe and Wise are no longer working together. In 1977 Eric proposed to his childhood sweetheart, Ann Bailey. They married and lived

very happily for a good two hours.
The set is a very inferior bedsit. Window with cracked and broken panes centre background, doors left and right. In the centre an old table and wooden-backed chairs. Ann is preparing tea at table. Eric enters. He is wearing shabby raincoat and cloth cap.

Ann Where've you been?

Eric My club in St James's.

Ann Anything doing down the labour exchange?

Eric Manager called me into his office.

Ann You got a job!

Eric No. He wanted to congratulate me – seems I've been going to that labour exchange for so long now I can go with them on their staff outing to Blackpool.

Ann *(Walks to mantelpiece and dusts it)* You've been out of work now for four years.

Eric You're not dusting that mantelpiece are you?

Ann What's wrong?

Eric I've planted potatoes in there! What a dump! Where's the television set?

Ann Men came from the rental firm and took it back.

Eric I once had my own television series now I haven't even got a set. Any other good news?

Ann Doctor says I'm going to have another one.

Eric I decide whether or not we have another telly, not the doctor.

Ann Doctor says I'm having another baby.

Eric Just what we needed, we've only got six, three sets of twins in four years.

Ann I can't help it.

Eric I've only got to look at you and it's a new pram.

Ann You'll have to get a job now.

Ann *(At the table with a brown stone teapot)* I've made a pot of tea.

Eric *(Crossing to table)* You bought a cup then?

Ann Found this plastic beaker in the cupboard.

Eric *(Picks up the plastic beaker from table and smiles)* It's the one Ern gave to us as a wedding present... bought in Reigate.

Ann Bought in Reigate?

Eric It's got on the side here BR.

Ann He even nicked a cup to give us as a wedding present.

Eric Had some great times with Ern. I liked him – we were like brother and sister.

Ann Doesn't want to know you now though, does he?

Eric Ern's a very busy man. TV star, president of four banks, not to mention his fourteen wig boutiques.

Ann rises, and stands behind Eric.

Ann Pansy.

Eric Pardon?

Ann The baby – think I'll call it Pansy.

Eric It might not be a boy. *(Laughing)* I can still come out with them, it's still there.

Ann If you're that good why don't you go back on the telly with Mighty Mouse and make some money?

Eric I've told you once I've got me pride. *(Sips tea)* They all think I've got it made. *(Sips tea again)* Make another pot of that tea and I'll do the doors with it.

Ann The rent's due today.

Eric Listen, Ann, when the rent man knocks you ...

Ann When he knocks I am not going to shout, 'They've gone on their holidays.'

Eric It worked last time. Five quid a week for this lot, I'll tell the rent man myself when he calls.

Ann Rent man won't be here, I wrote and complained and the landlord himself's coming to have a look.

Eric I wonder how he'd like to live here. I wonder if he'd like to share a bathroom with forty-eight other people. I climbed into that bath last Saturday night and I sat on that old fellow from upstairs ... and he was smoking his pipe.

Ann Get in touch with Ernie Wise and go back on the telly.

Eric No!

He bangs fist on the table top. The bedroom door falls off its hinges.

Ann Now look what you've done! *(Knocking at door)* Who can that be? *(Crosses to front door)*

Eric If it's Princess Anne tell her I don't feel up to a tour of East Africa just at the moment.

Ann opens the door and stares open-mouthed at Ernie, who is looking very affluent.

Ernie Hello, Ann.

Ann Ernie Wise!

Eric stands with his back to the door, trying to smarten himself up.

Ernie May I …

Ann Yes, come in.

Ernie enters room. Eric still has his back to him.

Ernie Hello, Eric.

Eric Ern!

Both shake hands warmly.

Ernie How are you, Eric?

Eric Oh, oh great, Ern! Fine … never been better. Sit down, Ern, take a seat.

Ernie Thank you.

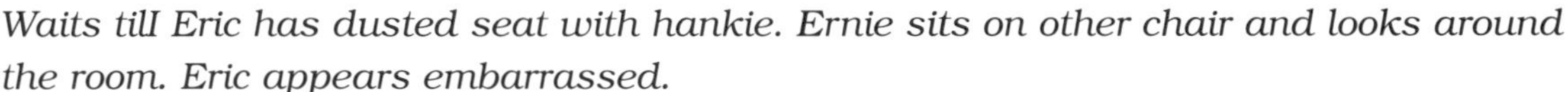

Waits till Eric has dusted seat with hankie. Ernie sits on other chair and looks around the room. Eric appears embarrassed.

Eric Ann and I were just taking tea, perhaps you'd like to join us.

Ernie Thank you.

Ann Would you like it in this cup?

She bangs the plastic beaker down in front of Ernie.

Eric Remember, Ern? That's the one you bought us when we got married.

Ernie Bought it in Reigate.

Eric *(To Ann)* I told you didn't I?

Ernie How are you, Ann?

Ann *(Very cold)* Couldn't be better, that three weeks on the Riviera did us the world of good.

Eric *(Embarrassed)* How are you keeping then, Ern?

Ernie Can't complain, Eric. *(Looking around)* It's erm … nice little place.

Eric *(Gets up, embarrassed)* Only temporary, Ern, only temporary.

Ann Any minute now, it'll fall down.

Eric You see, Ern, we are at the moment what you might call between houses.

Ernie *(Fully realises that Eric is in a bad way and tries not to embarrass him)* I understand, Eric.

Eric We're waiting for the men to finish decorating the big house that we've just bought, just bought a big house ... in the country ... you see.

Ann *(Slams beaker down in front of Ernie again)* Tea, Ern?

Eric *(Laughing)* Do you remember when we used to do that one?

Ernie I'll never forget those days, Eric. *(Raises beaker to drink tea)* Good health.

Eric *(Holds Ernie's drinking arm)* Not if you drink that.

Ernie *(Lowers beaker)* I still use some of our old jokes when I'm on the television.

Eric We never miss you when you're on. We're big fans of yours on the television. Often we say he's doing those old jokes.

Ernie *(Looking around for the TV set)* On the television?

Eric Yes. *(Embarrassed)* We did have one of those new thirty-inch colour sets only I asked them to take it back because it hurt Ann's eyes.

Ernie Sorry to hear that, Ann.

Ann They hurt most of all when you were on.

Eric My dear, I think I can hear Rupert crying.

Ernie Rupert?

Eric Our youngest girl.

Ann Excuse me.

She exits through opening where the door was.

Eric Lovely mover. Always was!

There is a short embarrassed pause after Ann's exit.

Ernie Well then, Eric?

Eric Well then, Ern?

Ernie How long is it now?

Eric How long is what now?

Ernie How long is it since we were together.

Eric Oh, about ten years. What do you think of Ann?

Ernie Oh, very nice.

Eric She's not at her best this morning. She's been out all night frightening policemen.

Eric You're looking well and doing well for yourself.

Ernie Yes. How about you?

Eric Oh. I'm fine, fine.

Ernie *(Looking round)* Fine, fine. *(Taking out wallet)* Eric, shortly after you left the flat I found this five pound note under the cushion on the settee, it must be yours because it was the end where you always sat. *(Offers fiver to Eric)*

Eric *(Knows it's charity but needs the fiver)* Thank you. *(Takes note and looks at it)* It is mine, I only ever had the one and it did have a picture of the Queen on it. *(Places note in pocket)* You're doing well for yourself then, Ern?

Ernie Not too badly. As a matter of fact the BBC have just offered me the biggest contract I've ever had, worth a lot of money.

Eric I'm really pleased for you, Ern.

Ernie Just one condition that they're insisting upon.

Eric I'm sure you'll be able to sort it out whatever it is.

Ernie *(Embarrassed)* Eric.

Eric Yes?

Ernie I was wondering... do you ever ... I mean ... would you consider...

Eric Yes, I must go now, Ern, business appointment in the City. I work in Throgmorton Street, I look after the frogs.

He rambles on to a shuddering halt.

Ernie Eric, come back with me, just like in the old days.

Eric No, it wouldn't work. People have forgotten me by now.

Ernie They haven't forgotten you! Honestly, people still come up to me in the street and say, 'Where's the fellow with the funny face?'

Eric Fellow with the funny face?

Ernie Yes. They haven't forgotten you. Come on, Eric, it's more fun when there's two.

Eric So I believe.

Ernie We could have our own show again. 'The Wise & Morecambe Show'.

Eric Wise & Morecambe.

Ernie I want to help you and Ann.

Eric I couldn't go back now, my timing's gone.

Ernie Once you've got it you never lose it.

Eric Four years ago I would have had an answer to that.

Ernie Try. One of your old tricks?

Eric OK. *(Slaps Ernie's cheeks and straightens his wig)*

Ernie Just as good as ever!

Eric You really think so?

Ernie What do you say? Just like in the old days?

Eric All right ... it's a deal.

Ernie I'm delighted, Eric.

Ann enters.

Eric Ann, my dear, what you've been saying all the time – I'm going back on the telly with Ern.

Ann I heard – 'The Morecambe & Wise Show'.

Ernie No, Ann, 'The Wise & Morecambe Show'.

Ann Oh, that little condition in the contract you had to sort out.

Eric Have you been listening again? No wonder they call you Jodrell Bank.

Ann Obvious, they've said to him, no Eric Morecambe, no contract.

Eric Is that right, Ern?

Ernie You're quite right, Ann, I think 'The Morecambe & Wise Show' sounds just fine.

Ann You haven't changed, Ernie Wise, self all the time.

Eric Oh yes he has changed. *(He holds up the fiver)* See this, Ern gave me this, said I dropped it in the flat but I didn't, he gave me this out of his own pocket.

Ann There's a catch somewhere.

Eric That's not a nice thing to say. Ernie is a changed man.

Ernie It doesn't matter, Eric.

Ann Give me that fiver. *(Takes note from Eric)* I'll give it to that landlord when he comes.

Ernie *(Takes note from Ann)* Thank you.

Eric What are you doing?

Ernie I am the landlord.

Back in Five

Ernie That's about it Eric, and I think excellent value.

Eric If you can get it for 5p I'll go along with that.

Ernie Some of my finest works between these covers.

Eric Some of my best work has been done in the same way.

Ernie Proud of that little lot I am.

Eric One thing puzzles me.

Ernie What's that?

Eric On the front of this book it doesn't mention you, some fellow called Eddie somebody.

Ernie Braben?

Eric That's her.

Ernie It's me. I use a pen name.

Eric So that's why I've never met him?

Ernie No such person – it's me.

Eric Have you got any plans for the future?

Ernie I'd like to do something with Des O'Connor.

Eric So would I but how can we lure him to the riverbank without him suspecting?

Ernie I think I've left something worthwhile behind me with those plays.

Eric Contented?

Ernie Very.

Eric What would you like them to put on your tombstone?

Ernie Nothing too grand, just 'Here lies the greatest writer that ever lived'.

Eric Not too much to ask.

Ernie What would you like them to put on your tombstone?

Eric Something short and simple.

Ernie What?

Eric 'Back in Five Minutes.'